Includes some short stories about our cottage on E Lake Blvd.
JW

Dear Cousins

Staying Connected the Old-Fashioned Way

Jean Hibbard Willett

Jean Hibbard Willett

"Old Pappy Time", by Stuart Hamblen ©1954 by Hamblen Music Co. All Rights Reserved. Used with permission.

"Dear Cousins," by Jean Hibbard Willett. ISBN 978-1-60264-421-2.

Published 2009 by Virtualbookworm.com Publishing Inc., P.O. Box 9949, College Station, TX 77842, US. ©2009, Jean Hibbard Willett. All rights reserved. No part of this publication may be reproduced, stored in a retrieval system, or transmitted in any form or by any means, electronic, mechanical, recording or otherwise, without the prior written permission of Jean Willett.

Manufactured in the United States of America.

Dedicated to Dann, my cheerleader, who never let me quit and who was always ready with a smile to try anything—all of which made him a loving husband, devoted father and exciting grandfather and to my grandchildren—to the first one who was my inspiration for the story, and also to the other eight whose stories fill these pages.

It may take a village to raise a child, but it takes a great number of family and friends to write and publish a book. Special thanks go to the daughter-in-law who listened to my problems week after week, to my nephew who experimented endlessly to get just the right cover and to my author team of three who kept me from getting depressed by the intricacies of working electronically when I was often not computer-friendly.

CONTENTS

PROLOGUE 1

CHAPTER 1
When a Child is Born So is A Grandma 3

CHAPTER 2
When You Can't Stand the Heat in the Kitchen 7

CHAPTER 3
A Revolving Door 13

CHAPTER 4
Winter Woes 17

CHAPTER 5
Newlyweds 21

CHAPTER 6
Exercise – But How Long? 25

CHAPTER 7
Twice Blessed 30

CHAPTER 8
Five Short Weeks 38

CHAPTER 9
Seven Long Weeks 42

CHAPTER 10
It's A Girl 46

CHAPTER 11
Outpost Fishing 54

CHAPTER 12
Flying Into the Sun 58

CHAPTER 13
Traveling Like a Turtle 65

CHAPTER 14
History Lessons 70

CHAPTER 15
Laddies and Lassies 76

CHAPTER 16
 Half Retired and Struggling 81
CHAPTER 17
 Sixty-Two and Counting 91
CHAPTER 18
 Over the Border 98
CHAPTER 19
 Fiftieth Anniversary – Ten Years Early 103
CHAPTER 20
 How To Retire 112
CHAPTER 21
 Over the Hill and Picking Up Speed 121
CHAPTER 22
 Wedding in the Wild 128
CHAPTER 23
 Traveling the Old Silk Route 134
CHAPTER 24
 New Year Traditions 139
CHAPTER 25
 Home Schooling 148
CHAPTER 26
 The "Green" House 154
CHAPTER 27
 The Big Hole 160
CHAPTER 28
 Are We Coming or Going? 168
CHAPTER 29
 The Eagle Has Landed 174
CHAPTER 30
 Spider House 178
CHAPTER 31
 Down Under 182
CHAPTER 32
 Home Sweet Home 191
CHAPTER 33
 Graduation Month 202

CHAPTER 34
School in Ireland 207
CHAPTER 35
Seeing Double 211
CHAPTER 36
In Sickness and In Health 215
CHAPTER 37
Call Home 222
EPILOGUE 227

AUTHOR'S NOTE

A Round Robin letter flies around unendingly. This Round Robin flew between seven cousins. In the beginning the Hibbard family was scattered throughout southern Wisconsin and northern Illinois. Being close geographically allowed frequent family gatherings most often on holidays. My father was third of six children so I had five Hibbard aunts and uncles. The next generation numbered fifteen children. Seven of those cousins were female. When the family spread beyond Wisconsin, the holiday parties ended and letters filled the void. At first letters, among the three oldest female cousins, flew from Michigan to San Francisco to Lake Geneva, Wisconsin. Two Racine Wisconsin cousins were added, then one from Florida. Lastly they added me living in Madison, Wisconsin. A fourteen year spread in age existed between Fran, the oldest, and me, the "baby". Each round travels approximately 7,000 miles. The bulky envelope contains seven letters, arrives every few months and fills my mailbox. Reading my previous letter allows me to review what I've written on the last round and to add a chatty new letter to bring the other six cousins up-to-date on my children, family joys and tears. The pressure of not letting down one's cousins eliminates procrastination and helps to send that letter promptly back into orbit. Seven Hibbard cousins have circulated this Round Robin for more than 57 years and kept us "kissing" cousins when miles intervened.

These tri-monthly letters constitute a sequel to *Dear Mom*, as the "never boring nor monotonous" daily events of our four sons inevitably changed with the next generation creating an extended family that included nine grandchildren. The letters, although full of laughter and tears, clearly show the challenges of retirement living, the need to set goals, and to repeatedly experience new learning experiences. Those nine youngsters, who tore through our house and our days, went home after daily visits or weekly ones thus enabling us to happily vacillate between being loving grandparents or curious retirees who had many ideas of things we still wanted to explore in our waning years.

The Seven Cousins

50 years ago   Now

Frances (Al)

Ede (Ken)

Georgiana (Bob & Butch)

Hope (Leonard)

Dorothy (Steve)

Lorraine (Bob & Wally)

Jean (Dann)

DESCENDANTS OF
Dann Willett, 1924–2008, and Jean Hibbard Willett, 1927–

Andrew Willett, 1951–
m. Linda Lyall
Anthony Willett, 1978–1999
m. Kayleen (Kate) Keefer
Alessandra Willett, 1986–
Aaron Willett, 1989–

Timothy Willett, 1953–2001
m. Bobbie (Margaret) Davenport
Martha Jean Willett, 1989–

Jason Willett, 1956–
m. Lynn Collins
Allison Willett, 1983–
Trevor Willett, 1986–
Elara Willett, 1988–
m. Sara Watson

Michael Willett, 1958–
m. Susan Hilliard
Lucas Willett, 1980–
Michelle Willett, 1984–

PROLOGUE

June 20, 1999

Dear Cousins,

I always thought grand parenting would be easy until we flew on our last overseas trip. We were thrilled anticipating another trip with the Friendship Force Weeks of preparation filled our days and then suddenly we were there. The Friendship Force works on the premise that "a world of friends is a world of peace" and one makes friends by living in the home of others. We home hosted with a young German couple in Jena, formerly behind the Iron Curtain. Delighted to find them online, we E-mailed messages home to all four of our sons' families. Prompt answers shooting back from the States energized Petra. Her internal software translator changed German to English or vice versa—okay as long as I did everything correctly. Some keyboard characters were placed differently which messed up my automated fingers. If the monitor asked "ja" or "Nein" I could not answer. The minute I deviated troubleshooting German instructions poured out. I would then continue by instinct, by prayer or holler for help causing difficulties when Petra was cooking dinner and stopped to rescue me.

The four of us spent five invigorating days exploring castles perched on every ridge, but the best trip occurred on Mother's Day. Driving to Dresden we scrutinized the palace grounds, toured the Zwinger and then squeezed back into the car after a long, exhausting day. As we started down the Autobahn the car phone buzzed, "Someone is trying to reach the Willett's. Call home immediately." By the time we reached our apartment, E-mail messages were coming through; "Call home" .We could think of only one reason why anyone would strive now for this extra contact with us. Our bonded extended family closes ranks easily. Which one was in trouble?

Dialing a long string of numbers suddenly a distressed son halfway around the world picked up. He told us that Tony, who is his nephew and our grandson, had been out with friends the previous night celebrating his 21st birthday. Tony's father had always stressed not to ride with anyone who had been drinking, so Tony told his friends he could not ride with them, but would jog home. After extensive high school cross-country participation, he could easily jog five miles down a country road. It was 2:00 a.m. He was almost home. A car, going in the same direction as Tony, flashed its lights at three oncoming cars to alert them to danger on the road. The first car slowed in response to the warning. The second car impatiently sped up and passed. That driver never saw Tony—only felt the impact.

CHAPTER 1

When a Child is Born So is A Grandma

April 30, 1978

Dear Cousins,

 We did it. We're now grandparents, but we stressed out getting there. I planned to fly to Houston as soon as that baby appeared because Andy would need help with his four-year-old step-daughter. Andy still works for IMCO, but his life took a drastic turn. Now instead of traveling worldwide to deal with drilling problems in Iraq, Alaska, or New Mexico, the company based him in Houston where he teaches candidates for mud school. Mud creates the lifeline of a well. Controlling this heavy fluid properly controls the well, but it takes a lot of training to maintain the correct consistency of the mud.
 Because I could stay only one week, it was important not to show up pre-maturely. Every day we fervently hoped that two events would not collide. Over the years we had acquired income properties mostly in downtown Madison. Recently we had added an apartment building in nearby Middleton. Because our lawyer worried about a fault in the abstract, each day he had pushed that closing one day later. When he reset the closing date for the fifth time, it fell on the baby's due date. Dann informed him I might have to leave with a couple hours notice. Needing my signature on the land contract, which had not been drawn up yet, the lawyer called us into his office Friday morning and I signed blank pages. Late Sunday night Andy phoned saying the birth was imminent. At 8:00 a.m. Monday he called again announcing that Anthony

Dann Willett had arrived. By mid-morning I was aloft. With a mile-wide grin, Dann strode into the closing at 11:00 a.m. and announced, "Good morning. Grandma Willett is not coming this morning."

Andy had purchased a house in Houston, but that deal also had been delayed. They had moved in only seven days before the baby came, so I arrived to mass confusion. The guest bed awaited me with only a narrow path to reach it. Stacks of unopened boxes were strewn around the rest of the room. By the end of the week that path had widened some, but I spent most of my time taking care of the baby and playing with his four-year-old half-sister. Texas stretches a long way away from doting grandparents and I went home reluctantly. This grandmother title thrills me— whatever it will entail.

Some time ago Dann decided that our four boys should acquire property while he, with his realtor's license, could help them. We didn't anticipate the flurry of activity this produced. The two sons in Madison, still living at home, began by looking for a two or three unit apartment building. Mike wanted one that he could move into in a year; Tim looked for one needing repairs that he could do himself. Dann took them to an investment clinic after which they sprawled on the living room floor nightly with clipboards and calculators. Dann culled listing sheets for them, as they calculated how to make each one a paying proposition. If we had had any more kids Dann would never get any paying work done.

Mike and Susan, his fiancée, are closing on their two-flat tomorrow. They plan on moving into one of their own apartments after their wedding next year. He became an eager landlord after receiving his first rent check.

While Dann has been making investors out of our sons, I've been creative on my sewing machine. I started making plaid flannel shirts—five at a time. My men all stand tall but skinny, so commercial shirt sleeves only stretch to ¾ lengths. If I increase to a larger size for more length, their shirttails make a good on-land sailboat. Measuring arm length, neck sizes and height I adjusted patterns for each guy. This eases the shopping at Christmas time. My enthusiasm overflowed with each success so I experimented on blue jeans for Mike. I took apart a pair of Levis beyond repair to use for a pattern. As that old pair fit really well, so did the new ones. Struggling without instructions created a challenge, but in the end they looked professional and the V-S tape stitching across the back pockets really impressed Mike. He calls that the Levi trademark. I'll let Levi do it from now on.

Tim and I have been working in Dann's rental management office. I handle the phone and organize the paperwork and Tim tackles the maintenance problems with each day providing a new challenge. Five rooms on the second floor of our building next door share a common refrigerator which stands in the hall. Yesterday one woman complained the newest tenant had been stealing her food. When I asked how she knew Mary did this, she obdurately responded, "I just know because of the guilty look on her face." The next day the first floor tenant reported that she had a knock on her door at 2:00 a.m followed by a male voice asking if she would please turn down her radio. We instantly connected. As we have no male tenants in that building and twice within the last two weeks we had found the side door to the basement unlocked, we concluded that a man must be living in the basement who was journeying up to the second floor at night to raid the refrigerator. Unwise of him to complain about that loud radio at 2:00 a.m. Dann, with two sons along as back-up, checked the basement and changed the locks.

While sitting in the office yesterday morning Tim studied his work list commenting that it doubled as the day progressed. Last week one tenant poured gasoline on the kitchen floor and ignited it claiming that this killed the cockroaches. We evicted him in a hurry and Tim gets to re-do that entire kitchen.

I commented he couldn't complain about a boring job. He responded, "You can say that again. It isn't every job that allows one to carry dead possums to the curb." I work part-time as naturalist consultant for the Madison School Board guiding five or six tours each week in the School Forest. I love being outdoors. I love working with children. Madison teachers bring their classes out for a half-day or an overnight and choose whatever phase of outdoor education correlates with their classroom work. I frequently teach mammal specials when working with the older classes and I needed a female opossum to demonstrate adaptations. Tim wouldn't even turn over that dead opossum to check its sex.

My chosen career of Occupational Therapy had lasted for only a year before I quit to cope with motherhood. When the last of the four boys entered kindergarten I went back to work, but instead of Occupational Therapy I followed different interests and this required additional learning. Mastering bookkeeping at Madison Area Technical College enabled me to handle our rental management office. Attending Arboretum classes qualified me as naturalist in the Madison School Forest. Now I'm not sure if I can handle two part-time jobs plus grandparenting.

CHAPTER 2

When You Can't Stand the Heat in the Kitchen

May 15, 1978

Dear Cousins,

We're remodeling our kitchen. I talked Dann into taking a week off so he can get a good start on this huge project. The remodeling was supposed to be a winter project, but it's now spring. We should be outside working on the yard and starting tomorrow my School Forest tours are booked solid.

Dann tore up my kitchen as we're replacing the stove and oven and adding a microwave. He will replace the counters and floors, darken the cupboards, change the hardware and add ceiling beams to create an early American look. We'll mount our New Haven antique wall clock plus an old kerosene lantern and use Grandmother Williams's six straight-backed caned chairs around an old oaken table. I value her chairs not only as antiques, but because my Grandmother (Anna Benson Sutherland Williams) bought them second hand from her sister-in-law Mary Williams in 1885, the year of Anna's marriage. After Dann rips out the stove and oven, he has four weeks to do all the carpentry and new floors before the new stove comes in. Some of this occurred while I was "grandmothering" in Texas. We do have an operating new microwave plus an electric fry pan, a crock pot and a coffeepot to heat water. Knowing this was coming, whenever I've baked for the past three months I've doubled the recipes. After returning from Texas I still found a cache of cookies, pie, cake and sweet rolls in the freezer. It takes getting accustomed to that microwave because if I'm off 30 seconds I court disaster. I burned up a plastic plate that I shouldn't have been cooking bacon on, and the dog enjoyed a potpie so overdone that I couldn't break it. I resolved to have NO company for the three months this might take—if I can stick to that.

We love dogs and have bred registered Brittany Spaniels often, but this time we ran into trouble. Cinnamon birthed one, stillborn. After four hours with no more puppies, we took her into the emergency clinic and they gave her a shot that produced another stillborn. The doctor felt there might be one more and prepared for surgery, but to be sure that a pup waited, she x-rayed the mother. This showed one more. She started to get ready for surgery, but right then Cinnamon dropped a live male onto the x-ray table. I periodically checked her all night. By morning Cinnamon was relaxed and we were dead tired and disappointed. We should just be thankful for a live mother and one noisy male, Ranger. Tim checked the pup at 6:00 a.m. this morning and said that pup has so many choices for lunch he won't be able to make up his mind where to go.

JULY 10, 1978

Dear Cousins,

When Mike graduated from Madison Area Technical College we planned a surprise party for him, but it surprised us. Sue and I had worked on this for weeks. We decorated a cake with an owl perched on top wearing cap and gown and clutching a diploma. We invited all Susan's relatives, all of ours in town plus some of Mike's friends. The guest of honor never turned up as he was detained at Madison General Emergency Room until 2:00 a.m. When he had come home from work earlier that day he had complained that something had gotten in his eye. I administered drops and he quickly showered, grabbed his robe and dashed out the door. After the graduation ceremony he announced to Sue that they had to stop at the Emergency Room. Dann and I drove directly home and found Tim holding the fort with a houseful of expectant guests. We all kept visiting while Sue, calling undercover from the Emergency Room, kept us informed every half hour. Two horrible auto accidents came in that night each time pushing Mike aside. After two-and-a-half hours we gave up and fed our guests—everything except the cake that we had worked so laboriously to decorate. At midnight the guests departed. Eventually the hospital removed a piece of steel from Mike's eye, doped him heavily for pain, bandaged his eye and sent him home. The next morning an eye specialist found and removed another piece of rusty steel. Mike's eye will be okay. Susan asked if we couldn't invite everybody over again just for that cake and ice cream, so we'll try again. A terrible arrangement as I'll have to clean my house twice.

Taking a two week vacation we drove through the Smoky Mountains camping as we went, and then spent four days checking on Jason our third son, who is studying for a semester in Washington, D.C., as a C.I.A. intern. He lives near the National Archives. Because I have been working on our family history I needed to research the year Dann's grandfather and family immigrated. They probably entered through Ellis Island in either 1884 or 1886—sometime prior to the birth date of Dann's father, which was August 5. We knew that Dann's grandmother was pregnant with Dann's father when they arrived, but we didn't know which year. His father never had a birth certificate and never knew the year of his birth. The Archival information includes census records, military service, land records and ship passenger lists. After hours of stiff necks scrunching in front of the microfiche I found the page that showed they came through Ellis Island, then called Castle Garden. They sailed on the steamship Forest Hill and arrived April 20, 1886. George Henry had been upset by the fact that they had lived in the shadow of Oxford in England, but his children would never be allowed to attend there. I believe the University of Wisconsin attracted him and he came directly to Madison.

We visited my brother in New Jersey, Dann's brother in Connecticut, and Dann's cousin, John Paul Hoxie, in Corning, New York. J.P. lived and breathed genealogy. He knew this intrigues me and talked us into going home through Canada to search out more Willett's. George Henry Willett, Dann's grandfather, had a brother Henry, who settled in Canada and had nine children. We found one named Ivy. When Dann said he was a relative, she replied, "I have lots of relatives I don't know, so come on out." Discovering lost cousins delighted her and she cried when we left. When I admired her oil paintings she promised to do one for us.

Our puppy, Ranger, chews everything in sight. When he knows he has been bad he rolls over, puts his feet straight up and bats his eyes. He digs in my plants, scatters dirt all over the carpet and loves to unplug the phone jack, usually when it's ringing, and then runs with it.

AUGUST 20, 1978

Dear Cousins,

Our friends, Rosemary and Walt, visited us at our cottage in northern Wisconsin and for five hours we canoed down the Brule River. Rosemary and I took the same canoe so we could bird watch. This put the two fishermen together in the other canoe. After reconnoitering just before some bad rapids, we paddled through perfectly. However at the quiet water end we hit a log that broadsided and overturned us. Dann and Walt paddled along shortly and tried to pick up belongings that hadn't been tied in—a canoe paddle and life preservers. In the knee deep water we emptied the canoe by rolling it. Rosemary and I had grabbed our lunches, which turned into sodden messes, instead of pulling out the more important binoculars. Dann and Walt spent their evening taking them apart piece by piece and spreading the parts out to dry.

Dear Cousins

Tim's birthday gathering this year included two Willett uncles with families. Tim had requested blueberry pies. We had difficulty placing 25 candles because a pie doesn't support candles. Uncle Don, Dann and Mike "horse and goggied" for the leftover piece. Susan did, too. She didn't know what she was doing, but wanted in anyway. This process consists of all interested parties holding out one clenched fist. The designated leader counts to three. At the count of three all fists open showing extended fingers—anything from zero to five. The leader totals the extended fingers and starting at his left he counts off including all who are playing. Wherever the count stops determines the declared winner. When Uncle Don won, everybody stared while he savored each bite, trying to make him feel guilty, but he didn't.

Susan and Mike have set their wedding date for one year from now and counting down the days—going to be a long count.

I have an incomplete, but workable kitchen and we have stopped trying to finish during the summer months. The microwave saves me. Shopped too long one day and didn't start supper preparation until 4 o'clock for 12 people coming at 5:30. I threw together two blueberry pies for the oven, mixed up a casserole, which took ten minutes in the microwave, and I was ready by 5:30. The nicest thing about the microwave is that it cooks for our staggered meals. I showed Jay how to operate it and told him if I got tied up at the office and didn't make it home for lunch, he could take his choice of leftovers in the refrigerator, fill a plate, cover with saran wrap and microwave for two minutes. When I arrived I found him sampling everything as he played with this new "toy". Tim and Mike sometimes put in ten-hour workdays and don't make it home until 8:00. The microwave makes it easy—also eliminates sticky pans.

I am not always an efficient cook, however. When we expected some college friends from out-of-town, I chose to cook a big turkey. I requested either Dann or Tim to come home for lunch to start the Weber grill and they did, but because work delayed me at the office Dann slowed it down by closing the vents. Murphy's Law started operating. (Everything that can possibly go wrong, will). I didn't discover until 3:00 that the charcoal had gone out because of the closed vents, so there sat a cold 12-pound turkey. Shifting it to a hot oven I frantically dumped more charcoal and starter fluid on the grill. Every time I went outside to see if the temperature had risen, Ranger grabbed houseplants and tore through the house carrying them upside down. The phone rang every ten minutes because nobody was covering the office and I had trouble answering courteously. Dann had said he would come home at 5:00 to help, but at 5:15 he called to ask what time was dinner and that was the last straw. I burst into tears and told him—never. He had called to say he had to make another stop before coming home, but instead he mumbled, "Okay, I'll be right there." Our guests arrived early providing us with a leisurely visit before dinner. This almost stopped me from inviting company for the rest of the year.

I guess most of you know that Dann finally caught his fish—an 18 ½ lb salmon. He caught it when we chartered a boat out of Racine and spent a half-day fishing with Georgiana and Bob. He couldn't wait to get home and show the boys—especially Tim. It took four days before I could gather the family together for a meal so we kept it on ice. For four days Dann showed it off to anybody who would look. We had to cut steaks off the tail because it wouldn't fit into my oven.

Dorothy, in your last letter you commented on feeling sorry for me with an incomplete kitchen for so long. It's not as bad as it sounds. The fundamental things are done, only finishing touches linger. My problem has been to create a modern kitchen that looked old. I do love to cook, even with an incomplete kitchen.

CHAPTER 3

A Revolving Door

SEPTEMBER 1, 1978

Dear Cousins,

The house now stands silent with Andy living in Texas and Jason leaving again—this time for his last semester on the UW Lacrosse campus. His packed car was something to behold. By the time he packed clothes, miscellaneous gear, considerable food that his mother sent so he wouldn't starve, his ten-gallon aquarium with the fish individually packed in plastic bags, his stereo with two big speakers, the aquarium stand, the six foot pole for his hanging plants and four big plants, he could no longer reach the floor shift. He would hold his stuff back with one hand while shifting with the other. As he drove down the driveway his parting comment drifted back to us, "Hopefully I won't have to shift often!"

That leaves two sons still at home, but actually Dann and I have existed all alone this week creating a totally different atmosphere. The carpets have stayed clean, the cookie jar level dropped slowly, we are still eating leftovers after a week, the dog sticks to me like a burr, the telephone almost stopped ringing and a car with gas in the tank always sits in the driveway when I want it. When we go to bed we can turn off all the lights and lock the door because no-one is still out. All because Mike and Tim went to Colorado to see if they could bring Tim's school bus back. After he quit UW-Stevens Point and traveled west, he bought a converted school bus, parked it in an old lady's field and used it for living quarters. Now that he's moving back home he wants to sell it, but can't when it is there and he is here. Retrieving it could create difficulties because Tim hasn't driven it for three years. Although the tires are bad, he can't afford new ones, so they are going to try without spares. The van, which Mike has been rebuilding for several years, was almost ready for its maiden voyage. The kitchen facilities weren't built in yet, but the tape deck, CB and bed were operable. Mike stashed tools in the storage bin to cover all conceivable problems. They departed with two extra drivers and with two kayaks strapped on top. Once they had departed, I kept trying to think about anything else. We knew they had left Colorado on Thursday so if we were to wake up Saturday morning with no bus or van in the yard, we could surmise they were stopped somewhere with problems.

A neighbor came over for coffee that Friday night. About 10:30 she said "I just saw lights come up your driveway. Are you expecting someone?" With an extra driver for each vehicle they had driven straight through. The kids had said to the bus, "Now git up and go" poured a little gas directly into the carburetor, jacked it up to get it out of the irrigated field and took off.

They tried to stick together, but in the process of changing drivers east of Denver they became separated. Mike didn't know whether Tim was ahead or behind him so he turned on his CB and said, "I need a location on a little green school bus with no ears that I've lost." He received three answers instantly and many more over the next ten minutes. Tim is painting it inside and out and building in bunks in hopes that he can sell it to hunters. We have sighed with relief that Tim's wandering days appear to be over.

Our youngest landlord is learning fast—struggling with water problems in the basement, plumbing that has to be replaced and tenants that argue about security deposits. But that rent check compensates for the problems.

Apparently we have had burglars. It took several days to piece things together. Thursday night we noticed a tiny hole in the porch screen door, just big enough to slip in a finger and push the bolt back. That did not provide entry because the door into the house was locked. I recalled that when I had come home from the office at 1:00 p.m. the dining room window stood open with a raised screen. None of us had opened it so we called the police. We had left for work at 8:00 that morning, but Dann came home unexpectedly an hour later and I came home early, right after lunch. We think that one of those times, the burglar was still in the house. Mike is missing all his old coins and many from his penny collection were strewn outside the dining room window. As Mike's bedroom overlooks our long winding driveway the burglar had ample warning to hastily retreat back through the dining room window and disappear in the woods. We changed the house key location and put new locks on all the first floor windows. This disturbs us that somebody wandered around in our house and most disturbing that one of us nearly walked in while this was going on.

Dann bought the house next door from an estate and placed a deed restriction on it to prevent that lot from being split. We enjoy the wildness and nature surrounding us too much to want to see a house on our boundary. Dann and Tim, and even I, have been dreaming of remodeling it in our "spare" time. This is lots more fun than sitting at a desk doing paperwork.

NOVEMBER 15, 1978

Dear Cousins,

Some time ago I agreed to be an alternate poll worker and when four last minute cancellations called in, City Hall asked me to work tomorrow. I was on site by 6:15 a.m. and worked for 16 hours. When I handled the registration table I often had to be hard-nosed about proof of residence for ten days preceding the election. Once the ten-day residence requirement stumped me. Two girls brought their lease to prove their new address. The lease was dated November 1 (Election Day was November 7), but they said their landlord had let them move in the weekend prior which added four days. The question was: are you a legal resident when you start paying rent (Nov. 1) or when you sleep there (October 28)? I finally declared them legal residents. We open the backs of the voting machines to tabulate and do everything twice to check for errors, always working in pair—one a supposed Republican, one a supposed Democrat.

February 8, 1979

Dear Cousins,

I am embarrassed at this time lapse. The quicker one answers this letter the easier it becomes. Conversely the longer it lies around, the harder it gets. I keep waiting for a big lump of time, necessary if I write a long letter. Mistake. Just write a short letter to keep it flying, but do it quickly.

Dann and I drove to Lake Geneva and skied at the Bunny Club. We went (1) because we had never been there; (2) because we had a coupon for a free lift ticket; and (3) to visit with cousins. You gals probably thought people only went there to gawk at the waitresses, didn't you?

Our house resembles Grand Central Station, but we can see the handwriting on the wall and suspect that in less than a year we'll complain because everything is too quiet. I cook a lot and rarely know whether we're having two for supper or five or more. Since the advent of her engagement Sue shows up almost daily. Tim teases her that she comes for supper oftener than he does. She sits at my end of the table and we spend each meal hashing over details for next summer's wedding much to the exasperation of the men of the house—especially Tim, as he thinks that's too far off to be planning details. I declared that it's about time for woman talk around the supper table to counter all the car discussion that's been going on for years. Doing things the hard way seems to challenge her—hand lettering invitations, constructing her veil using hand appliquéd lace and sewing the bridesmaid's dresses.

CHAPTER 4

Winter Woes

March 31, 1979

Dear Cousins,

    Jay graduated from Lacrosse in December and will be working for IBM in Rochester, Minnesota. He was offered a job in Washington, D.C., but we're glad that he's not going that far. One son away in Texas is enough. Jay decided to take some time off first and he drove to Houston to visit his brother coming back through New Orleans. Driving home he got as far as St. Louis when a storm forced him to stop at a motel. The next day he slowly slid through Illinois and called us late that night to say he had stopped at a motel again as the roads were closed with semis blocking the ramps. I realized that he was only five miles away from my cousin, but he said no way could he drive five more miles and under no circumstances would he leave the motel. By this time the temperature had dropped to -25 degrees. He needed to make it home the next day before the next forecasted storm, and he did, arriving mid-afternoon. It snowed for 2 ½ more days. Snow piles narrowed the streets. If cars parked on both sides, fire trucks couldn't squeeze through. Abandoned vehicles frustrated the plow drivers and they towed so many cars that they no longer had places to store them or to pile the snow.
    We had planned to split firewood that weekend as last summer we had accumulated a huge pile of downed trees. Dann rented a splitter for eight hours and Tim invited friends. Many couldn't get into town or up our long driveway through the snow.

Those that did couldn't leave for hours. They kept that splitter running all day so I just kept on feeding them. We now have an enormous pile of split firewood.

Jay stayed home most of January as his job didn't start until February 5 and we were grateful. Dann, Tim and Mike shoveled every minute they could fit around working or school, but Jay shoveled continuously. When the temperature warmed increasing the snow weight, the radio constantly warned about weight on roofs. Jay kept demolishing four-foot drifts on our garage roof. Most of it landed on the driveway for lack of any other place and had to be shoveled again. Dann and Jay drove downtown, and with Tim they worked on our many apartment flat roofs. Our dogs experienced big trouble and established a trail through the yard similar to the animal highways we find in the woods. If they stepped off those slightly packed trails, they would immediately sink until only the tips of their noses showed. The wild animals in the woods must be in real trouble.

Driving north, with Mike and Sue, to the family cottage for a weekend we experienced a true winter weekend when the temperature dropped to 20 below, which is what we always hope it won't do. To make matters worse our car heater died en route forcing us to travel for hours with no heat. Dogs cuddled on our laps creating heat and Dann took the down bags out of the trunk and fluffed them around us. Tim and his buddy also went up to the cottage on a different weekend. At -25 degrees his friend said he had never been so cold, but Tim loved it.

We haven't had any School Forest winter tours because the deep snow makes the trails impassable unless one has snowshoes or skis. However, guides do not rest in the winter. We set up a maple syrup operation in a city park. With 4th grade classes we tapped the big maples, collected sap daily, boiled it down over a campfire and sampled. This worked so well we offered public tours. At the end of the season we couldn't resist planning a guide's day out. The Dane County naturalist and I set up an early a.m. bird hike in the park and drafted our husbands to cook sourdough pancakes over a grill using our own maple syrup. I made my sourdough starter two days in advance and kept repeating the starter each morning so I would have enough to feed everyone. I decided afterwards that when Jesus fed the crowd with bread and fishes, he must have been using sourdough and the temperature must have been hot. I worried about having enough, but my starter just multiplied in the intense heat—not only ample to feed all the birders, but it spread like molten lava out of the bucket all over my car upholstery.

In spite of the weather our Thursday morning training lectures continue. I enjoyed the lecturer who talked about rehabilitation of wounded hawks and owls. People bring her almost 100 birds every year. She does surgery, splints broken feathers, administers antibiotics, exercises and feeds them while retraining them to catch their own food. She brought a great horned owl that she kept perched on her gloved hand cautioning us to sit still no matter what happened.

It's been a depressing week inundating me with cabin fever. Our tenants have been coming to us with personal problems that aren't our business. One tenant, Janet, has been threatening another one, Olive, with a knife. Yesterday both came into the office at the same time and started beating up on each other. I sent them home, but Janet came back later. I told her "I will answer your questions once and then you have to leave because I have to work." I did that, but she didn't leave, so I picked up the phone and called a friend hoping that Janet would take the hint. A friend of mine got an earful of make believe complaints to the police while Janet kept screaming in the background about my dumb, male, chauvinistic husband. She finally wore out and left screaming that Dann wasn't her friend anymore. Throughout all this Dann had sat quietly at his desk in the back office, but when she left muttering about us earth people uproarious groans spewed forth from his desk. I told him this qualifies me for hazard pay.

JUNE 30, 1979

Dear Cousins,

I have read all your letters a second time so I can answer your questions. The cottage I referred to, Dorothy, belonged to

Dann's folks. Each of Dann's brothers now owns one sixth. It stretches along the east shore of Lake Nebagamon 30 miles southeast of the city of Superior. In 1923, Dann's father bought the land that had been burned over and he, with the older boys, constructed this summer cottage. The family spent their summers there every year, except for "Pa" who stayed only part of the week and went back to the city on weekends to preach. This is the closest thing to a hometown that Dann has, as the Methodist conference moved their pastors around the state every four years. We have always spent our vacations there. Although it is a summer cottage we sometimes go for a winter weekend and call this survival. We heat with a wood stove but when the fire dies at night, it gets darned cold.

We had two Madison Area Technical College graduates this spring, Tim in surveying and Mike with an additional one-year course in woodworking and cabinetmaking. Mike refused to go to his graduation ceremony. He said last year was enough. We're really proud of Tim. After being gone for many years he came back and settled down to two years of studying. He became discouraged after sending out 25 resumes with no results, until the DNR called, offering a temporary job surveying lakes in northern Wisconsin. He will be moving around a lot and looks forward to hours and hours of fishing after work.

We've extended our fishing range. As some of you know, we, with Georgiana and Bob, chartered a converted tug boat for five days on Lake Nipigon. What luxury! We had bunks, a kitchen that usually wasn't level, a toilet although one had to bang on the wall to make the light go on, many fish waiting for us to catch them and a captain who cleaned all that we brought in. We usually caught our limit everyday and Georgiana and I cooked and ate fish constantly.

CHAPTER 5

Newlyweds

August 28, 1979

Dear Cousins,

Don't know if it's possible for me to write a short letter, but this bird needs to get on its flyway again. I have much to chatter about.

One evening last spring Dann realized that something was wrong with one eye so we stopped at the clinic. They admitted him to the hospital the next morning and he underwent detached retina surgery. They scheduled this for 8:00 a.m. and Dann didn't even miss lunch. They bandaged both eyes, but even blindfolded he would occasionally wander around his hospital room, which he wasn't supposed to do, and accidentally would get out in the hall. When you do this wearing only a hospital gown, it attracts attention fast.

After being home only four days, I took him to the emergency room with excruciating abdominal pain. At first we thought this related to the eye surgery, but after hours of tests the surgeon finally operated without knowing what was causing the problem. They found gallstones and removed his gallbladder. This time he did miss some meals and didn't work for eight weeks. Fortunately he recovered quickly enough that we could go on our annual Canadian fishing trip with Georgiana and Bob.

Mike and Sue's wedding stands out as our big event of the year. With my brothers' families, our immediate family, and out-of-state cousins, we housed a family of 13. It's handy to own the empty house next door and that's where we accommodated Georgiana and Bob. Unfortunately we didn't remember that we had turned off the hot water heater so they survived with cold showers. The younger boys slept in the camper bus. I don't think "Grandpaw Dann" will ever be the same since Andy's two-year old step-daughter, sleeping on a cot in our bedroom, woke up at midnight and sang to Grandpa "Little Bunny Foo foo hopping in the forest, swooping up all the field mice and bopping them on the head."

We catered the rehearsal dinner here the night before, and I prepared a big breakfast the day after including all the relatives. Sue and I had sewed for weeks making the groomsmen's shirts. Tim delighted in teasing Sue every chance he got saying, "She not only expects me to wear a suit, but a pink shirt yet." Sue insisted that shirt was peach, not pink. All three of Mike's brothers spent hours the day of the wedding looking for Mike's car, to no avail. It frustrated them when they discovered later that he had parked it on the Kayser Ford huge used car lot where they maintain a 24 hour security guard.

Mike and Sue had a rough July preceding that wedding. Their tenant had refused to move out and so the kitchen remodeling that was supposed to happen prior to the wedding, did not. The finished kitchen cupboards rested in our garage. They hired a lawyer, went to court, required the sheriff to serve a writ and hired a mover before they finally succeeded in removing the tenant. By that time only six days remained until the wedding.

We planned a different fishing trip with Georgiana and Bob this year, a one-day trip out of Racine harbor. Dann caught one of those big ones, but the story that goes with it is even bigger. The fish took a dive under the motor, which Bob immediately turned off. The fog wafted so thick around the boat that we couldn't see the huge boulders strewn close by along the shoreline. Dann hung over the back of the boat while he and Georgianna tried to untangle the propeller. Bob and I hung on to Dann's feet. After all that fussing the fish was still hooked, but barely and as Dann pulled the fish into the boat the plug fell out of its mouth.

P.S. Somebody messed up. Where is Ede's letter?

September 18, 1979

Dear Cousins,

    I am busy with School Forest tours and never should have laid this on my desk during guide season. I got up at 6:00 a.m. so I could finish it before I take to the woods.

    Tim drove to South Carolina to visit his friend who works with Vista. The trip was fraught with problems. His new, old car blew its thermostat and water pump on the way down. Having two problems simultaneously made diagnosis difficult. Coming back home the car malfunctioned again forcing him to leave it in a garage in Rockford, Illinois and he felt lucky to get that close to home. He called a friend in Madison, who called a friend in Beloit. They drove down and picked up the boys plus the cooler full of fresh crabs and shrimp and a tool chest that Tim was unwilling to leave behind. The Porsche rescue vehicle now had four people plus fish and tools forcing Tim to stick his head up into the sun window on top. They arrived home at 2:00 A.M. at which point I had to tell him that he had been moved up from 17th on the waiting list for the Wood Technics course and was expected in class at 9:30 that same morning. His friend Mary called that night to say she was okay, but 24 hours after Tim had left, the Red Cross Disaster Team evacuated the coastal island where she lives and works. Many wouldn't leave because they believe this to be an act of God and one can't run away from God. They sent Mary to another VISTA center 200 miles inland.

    Mike called yesterday asking to speak to the resident plumber. He had started tearing out the upstairs bath to repair the plumbing leaks under the floor when everything went wrong. He couldn't stop the leaks so he couldn't turn the water back on. When visiting cousins asked if they could see his apartment Mike announced only if they used our bathroom first. Dann added his expertise and they worked most of the night, but both came home discouraged. Every time they got something fixed, something else leaked. Mike has worked only half through the list of building code violations and has 30 days left before the deadline.

Over Labor Day Dann helped him put outlets in the bedroom, which had none—bad when one has a heated waterbed.

OCTOBER 24, 1979

Dear Cousins,

Okay, ladies, NO fish stories this time...well maybe just a brief one. We invited six people for supper to help us eat Dann's big Chinook. After we had all eaten until we felt stuffed we walked up the road to the Owen Conservation Park and hiked through the silent woods in pitch blackness. No flashlights allowed. Not the usual type of dinner invitation, but I'm sure they will talk about the absolute silence and beauty of the night woods for a long time. I did warn them in advance to dress appropriately. After 20 minutes of no lights your eyes will adjust, allowing you to see more. It's essential, however, to have faith that your guide knows the trails and the way out.

Some of us who work in the School Forest are considering enrolling in an exercise class. A University professor is researching the loss of calcium in elderly women and its relationship to exercise. He's looking for elderly volunteers—over 35! After complete physicals they would set up an exercise program for the participants. Sounds great, but wait until you hear the rest. This program requires a 45-minute exercise class at 7:00 a.m. three times a week for four years. I just don't know if I could face that 7:00 a.m. stuff.

Hope, I hope you didn't catch any of that hurricane that ripped through Florida.

CHAPTER 6

Exercise – But How Long?

December 18, 1979

Dear Cousins,

One December highlight was a wedding reception complete with dancing. Nobody was out on the floor until Dann said, "This is jig music like we listened to in the hills of Arkansas and loved." He stood up and started to jig in our little corner and reached out for Bobbie, Tim's girl friend. They circled around faster and faster. Although they danced off at one edge of the room they became the center of attention, getting rounds of applause that I don't think they even heard. Have you ever watched people jig? Their feet go so fast you can hardly see them move. This performance impressed us, but he delivered a punch line when he leaned over and whispered in my ear, "I have to go to the bathroom. I think it's imperative to take off my long johns."

I have committed to this university research osteoporosis study. They will try to determine a correlation between exercise and calcium decline and have chosen 120 women between the ages of 35 and 65. We ran a gamut of medical tests, EEG, treadmill stress tests, x-rays, and bone scans before they accepted us.

I have to be at the Natatorium on Campus by 7:00 a.m. Mondays, Wednesdays and Fridays for four years. When we go out of town the instructor provides a special program so we don't miss days. When we went camping I spread the dog rug out on the blacktop road for my exercises appreciating the fact we were alone in the state park. Things got difficult when we reached Andy's in Denver, as his four-year-old step-daughter couldn't concentrate on getting ready for day care when Grandmother was lying on the living room floor kicking, running up and down the stairs or doing a dance routine in the kitchen. When I jogged around in the backyard five dogs accompanied me.

Several of us car pool to the Natatorium. We complain all the way and that makes us feel better. Our project director has a background in physics, physical education, anatomy and dance. We do stretching and warm-up exercises until we reach our target heart rate. This means until you are ready to drop.

I keep telling myself how good this must be for me. It will be nice if it causes some needed weight loss, but I think it will just rearrange. I survived my first stress test. They placed a mouthpiece in my mouth so that I am breathing a controlled air mixture and can no longer speak. Establishing a code they periodically ask how you're doing. If I raise one finger it means I'm fine, two fingers means I'm getting tired, three fingers means please stop as soon as possible, four fingers means stop immediately. Every two minutes they tilted the treadmill up again to make me walk more uphill. I wondered what would happen if any of us broke a bone during these four years and we found out. One woman broke her ankle playing tennis and she came on crutches and exercised her arms and one leg. One fringe benefit is my new breakfast cook. When I return home at 8:05, Dann has breakfast waiting.

Georgiana, we're anxious to hear about your trip to Norway and wonder if that frozen salmon, which you were taking for your daughter, actually arrived still frozen after it got lost for three days in transit. And how did you manage to cook for 42 kids when they only spoke Norwegian? For a working gal you really get around. I think you have an understanding boss and a husband with itchy feet.

August 12, 1980

Dear Cousins,

Dorothy, your Hawaiian trip sounds fabulous. My idea of retirement is to be free to travel like that although most of you seem to manage it before retirement.

All summer I have been either getting ready to go away or trying to catch up afterwards. Our annual fishing trip to Canada with Georgiana and Bob was fun and lucrative. Traveling on a converted tugboat up and down Lake Nipigon gives one only a small deck space for exercises, making one embarrassed when other fishing boats pass by.

Having Tim with us this year made it special because he kept getting excited. He claimed, "Nobody told me to bring equipment to catch whales with." He is content to fish and fish and fish and I eat fish similarly, which makes a good combination. Georgiana and I make an important part of this crew because we happily eat fresh walleye all day long, even at midnight thus keeping us under the daily limit and legal.

In July we took an extended week at the family cottage at Lake Nebagamon in northern Wisconsin. Over the weekend we added three sons plus one spouse as they wanted to kayak on the Brule River. One's family actually never gets smaller, just stretches. I fed an army and no matter what I put on the table it melted away. Fresh fish appeared often and frequent blueberry pies using wild blueberries picked from the back swamp.

We arrived home with barely enough time for me to get ready for 4H camp at Upham Woods in the Wisconsin Dells. I have been a nature counselor there for 11 years, but this has to be the last as it exhausts me and comes at a time when Dann needs me in the rental office. We registered 120 kids and struggled with constant discipline problems. When I plan and execute programs all day from 6:00 a.m. to 10:00 p.m. I don't appreciate getting up at 2:00 a.m. to prevent cabin raiding or tent stake pulling. One night we always camp out on Blackhawk Island and take hourly shifts all night recording night sounds. I crawled into my sleeping bag about 2:00 a.m. only to wake at 4:30 with gentle rain washing my face. I don't worry if the girls get wet, but we were camped on a sandbar exposed to potential thunder and lightning. With no trees and 35 girls I couldn't string tarps. We had anchored the camp barge, necessary to transport us back to the mainland, close by our site. Neither the other site of girls nor the boy's site could leave until I showed up with the barge so I couldn't debate long, but I did not want to move sleepy girls through pitch black woods to get to the barge. I decided to send my disturbed junior counselors back to their sleeping bags to stay dry as long as they could because I needed another half hour to gain some beginning daybreak and I calculated the lightning was still far enough away. By 5:00 a.m. sleepy girls, with bedrolls thrown over their shoulders, followed me stumbling down the narrow woods trail to the water. By a quarter to seven the barge transported the last site of boys across the old channel in pouring rain, but nobody minded being wet as we were going home that morning anyway. Dann complains that it takes days for me to rest up after one of these weeks.

 I must admit to having great difficulty performing my exercises while at camp as I usually get up at 5:00 a.m. and fall in at midnight. I anticipated this and cheated. As camp lasted only four days I did two extra ones before I went and two extra after I came home. Fran, in answer to your question as to why I do this, I wonder about that myself. I come home exhausted. The "why" should be self-explanatory. Dann says he can see I have more energy. I have fewer back problems. After half a year, it doesn't get any easier to get up and go. It takes time that I don't have so it's a good thing that I go with friends. We egg each other on.

 Mike and Sue are now four weeks away from their due date and Mike has been ripping out walls in their apartment in order to make a second bedroom. Everything is thoroughly messed up.

Dear Cousins

It's going to be a tight race which gets here first—the baby or the second bedroom. They took a hospital tour yesterday and told us about special grandparent visiting hours when we can come and hold the baby. Happy summer to you all.

CHAPTER 7

Twice Blessed

OCTOBER 12, 1980

Dear Cousins,

    Yes, we are grandparents again. Lucas Michael arrived three weeks early. Mike, his father, had just torn apart walls and doorways to create a second bedroom, which made a terrible mess. Susan and the baby were hospitalized for ten days because of a bilirubin problem and then went home to her parents for a few days while the new father worked frantically on that second bedroom. Thankfully Mike has brothers, cousins, father and father-in-law as he needed them all. It's also good he has that hands-on attitude no matter what he's working on, just like his father. Since age 12 Michael has been delving into the innards of cars and he has followed a straight course from taking apart automobiles at Madison Area Vocational School to working in an auto body shop with dreams of some day having his own shop.

    Getting up for exercise class does not get any easier. I had thought it might. My work schedule prohibits the car pool so I no longer have sympathetic ears listening to my complaints. Also it's hard to get moving when it's still dark.

    Tim was the only one still living at home, but he has once again left and will be living with surveyor friends leaving Dann and I alone, for the first time, in this big house. I am taking advantage of the empty rooms to do some much needed decorating. We designated Tim's old bedroom as our winter bedroom because of its fireplace, so now I often read in bed in front of a glowing fire. This bedroom faces south. The one we have always slept in faces north and we closed it for the winter. I made insulated window coverings, called Roman Shades, for the windows. The cold gets trapped between the window and the Roman Shades and greatly improves our drafty house. I taught my Homemakers how to make the shades as people are beginning to realize the need for energy savings. I have been active in Dane County Extension Homemakers for many years. My life has been full of varied learning experiences and this is truly continued education. On a given day each month the Extension office provides leader training for the selected topic for two members from each of the 20 clubs within Dane County. Those two then return home and teach their entire club. "Teach one to teach more" is a powerful teaching concept. I remember the first lesson that I attended many years ago on how to putty windows and fix dripping faucets. I wasn't too happy with that topic and never admitted to any of the males in my family that I could do it.

Dann and I are in charge of a turkey dinner planned to boost our desperate church finances. I do enjoy this. Perhaps my bossy nature likes parceling out work to others. I made a plea in church explaining the need and how we could only manage to do this if everybody shared their talents. Apparently people reassessed their talents and many volunteered time, but the most surprising offer was 100 pounds of potatoes that appeared the next day. Unfortunately we don't use real potatoes, but gifts of talent cannot be turned down, so we found a way. We served 191 pounds of turkey making a profit of $1,300. Susan helped wait on tables and when she and Mike stopped to eat, I took the baby and walked around the dining room directing operations with Lucas on my shoulder. It was difficult to supervise when people kept trying to snatch him away.

Two of our friends are retiring and will move to Florida. I worked with and under her for years as I pursued my naturalist training. She and I, with husbands, have camped and canoed together often. The idea of retiring and having leisure time begins to appeal more and more, but I wish all my friends would stay close by.

We finally sold the house next door and that closing was an epic. We issued the renters a 30-day notice from August 1, but offered a bonus if they would move by August 15. The buyers wanted to move before school started, but the renters declared they couldn't possibly leave early. Because Monday, September 1, was Labor Day, we set the closing for Friday, August 29. Because of the holiday the buyers hired movers for Saturday the 30th and the renters had agreed to this. However on the night of the 27th they still hadn't found any place to go. The buyer's lawyer decided to hold back cash at the closing in case the renter wouldn't move out. This angered Dann and he declared, "No way. I won't allow any escrow because the offer doesn't call for it."

If the renters were not out by Sunday night the lawyer was probably going to sue us anyway and until Sunday night, the 31st, we hadn't done anything wrong. The lawyer responded by threatening to pull Dann's license. The closing, on Friday afternoon, was a comedy of errors. The title company had posted somebody else's entries on the abstract, the taxes showed up incorrectly as unpaid, the mortgage company gave us two different balance due figures, the new deed didn't match the mortgage because the old easement still showed although we had eliminated it. By the time all these corrections had been made it was late afternoon. Everything had to be recorded on Friday or all the figures would change, so the bank president took the payoff checks and rushed to the City County building. Our lawyer left, but returned immediately holding an envelope he had found lying in the street containing the payoff checks that the bank officer apparently had dropped. We tried to locate him as we thought he must be frantic. When we finally reached him he said, "You won't believe this. My car has just been towed away." In his haste he had parked in a "no parking after 4:00 p.m." zone.

The moving van arrived Saturday morning. The renters were not out and the moving crew sat for five hours. Eventually their foreman sounded off at the renter who got angry right back. At that point I reminded the buyers that, inconvenient as it was, the renters were moving 24 hours before they had to and it behooved everybody not to upset them too much. I kept feeding people hot sweet rolls to cool things down.

I entertained my sewing circle for lunch yesterday and In the middle of lunch I looked up to see a little old lady who had just walked in the front door, her arms loaded with packages. She stood in the middle of my living room and plaintively asked, "This is the place, isn't it?"

I said, "Sure, this is the place. What place?"

"The president's house," she replied in a confused manner. She was looking for the University President's estate, just up the hill. I offered her lunch, but she chuckled and left.

MARCH 31, 1981

Dear Cousins,

We listened in horror yesterday to the attempted shooting of President Reagan. That sick young man makes me lose faith in the human race.

We had bad news of our own as we have just come back from nine days in Denver trying to help Andy. He has filed for divorce and will have full custody of three-year-old Tony. This has been inevitable for some time. Now perhaps things will improve.

One of Dann's great nephews was baptized at church yesterday. Dann's brother, who is the baby's grandfather, performed the service and talked about how important this church has been to the family. Starting with George Henry, Dann's grandfather, who emigrated from England and was an original trustee, down the family tree to Dann's father, who was pastor here at one time and lastly to our grandchildren who are 5th generation.

Jean Hibbard Willett

AUGUST 20, 1981

Dear Cousins,

This is a grandmother's missile this time around. Congratulations, Lorraine, for joining the ranks. I like this grandmother title and enjoy the little ones when they're good, but hand them back quickly when they're not.

My exercise class is scheduled for four years Fran with two-and-a-half left to go. You're right about running out of steam. It ought to get easier, but that's a big time commitment each week. As we get older I think it gets more and more important to keep moving our joints. You all have an open invitation to go with me any morning any time.

Our family is expanding again. Jason was married in June, in Rochester, Minnesota. Andy, with his young son, flew out from Denver for the occasion. I thrilled to see our four sons dressed up, which occurs only at weddings. Our two grandsons wore matching suits and vests that Susan and I had made. Unfortunately when leaving home, Luke was picked up directly from his crib and laid in the car. Nobody noticed his bare feet so that eight-month-old grandson attended the wedding in formal suit and vest but with bare feet.

Our Canadian fishing trip with Georgiana and Bob this year was filled with problems. Fog submerged us the day we were supposed to return. We were at the other end of Lake Nipigon far from home base. The captain said he could maneuver in rain, winds or darkness, but not in fog. Time kept marching on. We were due back Sunday afternoon, and he had another charter going out then. The fog kept shifting and the captain kept trying. He would lift anchor and we'd be surrounded by endless water when suddenly fog would again cloak us solidly, forcing him to plod on until he could find a safe harbor. Four times we stopped. Four times we started again. The last time we were beyond any possibility of stopping so we continued in both fog and darkness. The captain called Tim up to the wheelhouse and showed him how to run the boat. More importantly, how to stop it. He gave Tim a heading to keep and a flashlight to read the compass by, and then doused all the lights. Leaning over the bow the captain fervently searched the water ahead for islands or reefs. Georgianna and I went to bed. I hated to miss all that excitement, but thought somebody should get some sleep before driving home. We docked at 1:00 a.m., 10 hours late. Hastily moving our gear to the car all our men then curled up in the backseat and collapsed until dawn. When Georgiana saw the kind of weather I was driving in, she stayed wide awake.

JANUARY 15, 1982

Dear Cousins,

Mike called during supper last night and said, "Let me talk to Pop quick." He had been keeping the thermostat in his building down to 50 degrees in order to conserve and also had turned off the heat in the front hall. Temperatures had dropped over the weekend. The wind added a bad chill factor and blew the plastic off the front door further chilling the front hall. When Mike and Sue came home from the Laundromat they could hear what sounded like somebody taking a shower. As they walked onto the front porch, water poured out the door freezing as it hit the porch. Mike shut the water off, discovered that the hot water pipe in the upstairs bathroom had frozen and burst creating a waterfall down the stair, which had soaked the wiring. His father-in-law took apart all the circuits in order to dry them. The shock factor finding a waterfall when they had arrived home was greater than the resulting bills.

I can hear what Dorothy is saying about this Wisconsin winter weather. We have been confined so many weekends they won't even know us at church. I do enjoy the snow, but the chill factor is something else. Tim drove out to Denver to visit, got caught in mud and rock slides and couldn't get through because of road closures. He commented, "With a chill factor of -50 there isn't a can of Heat or pair of long johns for sale anywhere in town." For those of you not from Wisconsin we have had a chill factor of -70 for the last two weekends. The first time when the forecasters warned us everybody seemed to think they didn't mean us. Stranded cars clogged all the streets. So many pipes froze that the plumbers would not come except for burst pipes.

When the forecasters warned us a second time stores jammed immediately with people stocking up on groceries, kerosene heaters and battery cables. By the time the temperature actually dropped, streets were deserted. Mike and Sue had driven to Denver to ski. Driving home Mike said that when they stopped for gas and to check the skis on top of the car, they couldn't stay out in that cold long enough to do both. They stopped at a Country Kitchen in Cedar Rapids, Iowa and were not allowed to leave for three hours until a plow came through and everybody caravanned behind it. When I asked them over for dinner this weekend they accepted, depending on the weather, saying if it was that cold again they wouldn't even drive across town.

Lucas was divided between his grandparents for the ten days they were gone. His grandfather taught him the barred owl call so he goes around the house hooting at us and this has earned us the permanent title of Grandma and Grandpa Owl. Although we enjoyed Luke, Cinnamon and Ranger, our Brittany Spaniels got tired of the kid and remained only tolerant. I taught the two dogs the meaning of the word turns. Commanding them to sit I would place dog treats in my outstretched hand simultaneously saying "Turns". Both dogs would sit patiently and would only gently take a treat if I called her or him by name. Before long I discovered three bodies were sitting expectantly before me.

Last fall we drove to Florida, camped coming and going and visited our friends, who have retired to Ft. Meyers. The highlights of the trip were the bird sanctuary on Sanibel Island

and a canoe trip in the northern part of the state. We rented a canoe and paddled down what looked like a jungle stream. I searched for alligators all day. I thought they were probably searching for me, but I didn't find any. Florida is a long drive home.

My exercise class has passed the halfway mark. Twice I have just rolled over in bed because of bad weather. I can't see going out at 6:00 a.m. not knowing if the car will keep going and expect Dann to rescue me at that hour. A Cable TV team televised the class one morning and we began getting calls from Washington State and Texas that we were on TV. Most of the class missed seeing it because we were in class. I gave a talk on the Osteoporosis program to my Homemaker Club and that inspires me to keep plugging—no more rolling over in bed.

The doctor talked to our class yesterday. He has applied for another five-year grant and estimates they have spent $1,000 apiece on 120 of us. I can't believe they'll let this nicely controlled group of women escape after four years. And yes, I have to exercise while I'm in England. Twice a month, on random days, we have to fill out diet sheets. I don't know what their computer is going to do with things such as Yorkshire pudding and steak and kidney pie. The little boxes on the diet sheets don't even come close to describing anything like that.

Gals, Georgiana is trying to encourage me to write that Dear Mom book I always dreamed about by giving me a book entitled HOW TO WRITE A BOOK, but I'm beginning to think it's hopeless. Where is all this free time we're supposed to have after the kids fly the coop?

My apologies for keeping this warm and safe for too long.

CHAPTER 8

Five Short Weeks

APRIL 15, 1982

Dear Cousins,

Just a short note so you don't forget about me. The day after tomorrow Dann and I are leaving for our five-week vacation to England. I hate to think of this Round Robin sitting here waiting, so please skip me this time around.

We've wanted to go to England for a long time. Dann always said after he pays all that money to go somewhere, he's not coming right back. We hope to do much hiking and some genealogy. Yes, Lorraine, I will be researching the Hibbard's, specifically Robert Hebard who immigrated to American in 1635. Thank you for that contact address. We'll also be looking up some Willett contacts.

AUGUST 26, 1982

Dear Cousins,

I feel out of the swim after missing one round of letters. Yesterday I flew to Denver to return Tony to his father and he and I have been busy reading and making cookies. This will be a short trip as I turn around and fly home tomorrow. We had Tony in Madison for a month, but we also kept Luke for a week because his parents were backpacking in the Porcupines. The boys, now aged two and four, were delighted with each other. Being a single parent is tough, but Andy is doing well both with his super active, small son and with keeping house.

I am apprehensive about all the expectant remarks on our England trip and hesitate to subsidize the U.S. postal system. Yes, I did keep a journal, but. Dann commented that writing about 34 days is too long for anybody to read. To the contrary, we have found our house guests unable to put it down and it has already traveled to Texas and New York. If anybody is interested I'll send it direct to you to read and return.

No matter what we did, all was exciting as I had never been overseas. On our last day as we traveled back to London via coach we were unable to get seats together. I sat next to a lovely lady who asked what one thing about our trip was most memorable. I couldn't answer her question, but pondered it on the long flight home and realized the answer is—the people. Perhaps it was the manner in which we traveled, which constantly put us in contact with people who went out of their way to advise us. The most valuable gift one can give anyone is time and I could not reciprocate the time given to us by strangers. We traveled by coach because we thought we would see more and we stayed in Bed & Breakfasts. We left our excess luggage in London, including dress clothes, and traveled only with backpacks.

We had no set itinerary and when we went into an area we would stay three to five days exploring by foot or local bus. Starting in London we moved briefly through the center of England to Scotland, down the coast to the Isle of Man and back through the Cotswolds. We usually ate in pubs where the food was good, but cheap and the socialization endless.

We have great memories of people. One set of Bed & Breakfast hosts took us to a Tory coffee hour to help support Maggie Thatcher. They introduced us to the village mayor who told jokes I didn't get. One B & B hostess thought some of her guests were using too much hot water so she removed the plug for the tub. The Bed & Breakfast hostess in Leeds led us across the city at 7:30 a.m. back to the car rental so that we could return the car in time to catch the 9:00 bus. She knew we had not been able to follow directions the night before when we had driven around lost for two hours. The black bus conductor in London gave me a sermon on how people should be more like flowers and give out more love. The second cousins we found in Yorkshire were unique. We knocked on their door and announced we were descendants of George Henry Willett from America. She responded "I don't know who the hell you are, but come in anyway." The B & B hostess in Bath wrapped Dann's pajamas around a hot water bottle. We didn't discover for hours that the bottle leaked making it imperative to wake her up in the middle of the night. Travelers love to compare notes and as we continued to travel people often asked for recommendations for places to stay. We sent them all to our Bath lady and said "tell her that her leaky hot water people sent you." The man in the Pump Room at Bath who shared our table really annoyed me. After a discussion on free medical care and college education, I commented that I thought people valued things more when they worked for them. He upset me when he answered, "Well, all women think like that". We loved the possible cousin on the Isle of Man who was a Cannell, as was Dann's grandmother. She allowed us to take her to the old Primitive Methodist church where Cannells had attended for generations. The sign out in front stated "Church services upon demand". The total attendance, including preacher and organist, was only 10 people. Our B &B host on the Isle of Man arose at 6:00 a.m. to make us a hot breakfast before we boarded the 7:00 a.m. back to England .The senior naturalist at the Winchester Nature Reserve gave us a personally conducted tour over the premises and took us home for high tea. Our meticulous hostess in Oxford polished her brass thresholds daily. We stepped over them with equally meticulous care. People everywhere asked what America thought about the Falklands and why President Reagan didn't do something. We were not about to defend the United States government, but we adored all the people who made our days so pleasant. Although strangers, they invariably treated us like family giving of their time without hesitation.

 We walked 10 miles/day so it didn't matter how good or bad the beds were. By the time we dropped into them, we welcomed anything. I missed some exercise days because I was too tired, but I filled out my computer diet sheets and they were dillys. I wish I could have heard the comments when the instructor checked them over.

We spent a lot of time on genealogy research. I failed with my Hibbard inquiries. At Salisbury, we were told that the records were in Trowbridge, but when we got to Trowbridge they told us the records were in Salisbury and we couldn't go back. Researching the Cannell's on the Isle of Man was also tough, but we had great success with the Willett's. We walked the streets of the little country village where Willett's had lived for over a hundred years. We saw the house where Dann's grandfather, great-grandfather and double-great had lived. It probably still looks the same. Sitting in the pub we learned all the village history, the origin of the Wesleyan Methodist chapel where Dann's great-grandfather was a lay preacher. Enough, but you all have an open invitation to come see Dann's slides.

CHAPTER 9

Seven Long Weeks

FEBRUARY 3, 1983

Dear Cousins,

With very little warning last fall Andy's company transferred him to Williston, North Dakota putting him in charge of the district office. He called and asked if we could take Tony again while he worked through the moving process. We met in the Minneapolis airport, transferred the child and Andy flew back home on the next flight. He put his Denver house on the market and moved into a Williston motel. Fortunately, his Denver house sold immediately. He purchased a new one in Williston and put his name on a waiting list for a daycare center. However it took seven weeks for that house deal to close and for an opening in the day care to materialize.

Surprisingly we managed well during those seven weeks. It was guide season so I needed a day care center close by. The woman agreed to take Tony on an hourly basis, as my guide schedule swings from zero to eight hours on a given day. We agreed that I wouldn't give up working while Tony was with us, but we would give up any functions that couldn't include him.

With glee I used him as an excuse for anything that I didn't want to do. We see him so seldom that we wanted to spend time with him. He's now five, but hyper-active and requires much one-on-one attention. So we dug carrots, raked leaves, made Halloween cookies, jack o'lanterns and ghost costumes. We took him to choir practice where he alternately sat in the laps of the altos and basses. He and the dog ran circles around each other, but every three days he reminded us that he couldn't stay for always, just for a visit. A couple of times toward the end he complained of not feeling well. Judging by the speed with which he would tear around minutes later, we chalked that up to homesickness and that's not bad for a five year-old. Every Tuesday night Lucas came for supper and stayed overnight as both his parents had class that night. We tucked the boys in together and they would lie awake and talk. I think Tony was thrilled with relatives that constantly popped in and out. Living with just a single Dad this kind of people traffic probably never occurs at his house.

We drove him home just before Thanksgiving staying overnight at Jason's in Minnesota. In the morning when we were concerned about a worrisome oncoming blizzard, we lifted a sleeping, pajama-clad Tony into the car at 6:00 a.m. By 7:00 we were in the ditch. Passing cars immediately stopped to help; I took off Tony's pajamas (not a good thing to travel in, in the wintertime) and shifted to winterized clothes. Dann reduced our speed to 25 miles an hour and we continued west. Tony continually and apprehensively asked, "I am going home today, aren't I?" In the midst of the storm, we pulled into a pancake place crowded with truckers. Waiting a long time for our pancakes because the owner was holding the fort alone, Tony happily circulated throughout the café telling everyone with great delight, "I am going home today." I began to wonder.

We asked the truckers about the weather and they said, "If you're going east, stop. If you're going west you'll drive through it in a bit." And so we continued west for hours arriving only a few hours after the movers finished settling Andy into his new house.

It was close to midnight when with great relief we told Tony, "Yes, we did take you home today." We unpacked hundreds of boxes, I cooked up a storm to leave behind, Dann fixed all those little things that never work at first and we left two days later.

With Tony gone we made up for lost time with our Christmas parties. I have discovered an efficient way to entertain is to clean the house thoroughly and to have consecutive parties. We hosted three one week. That way we don't have to put away chairs or dishes and the decorated house looks festive. We had the square dance club for the third time. As our reputation grows, the party keeps growing. I set tables for 60 guests this year stretching us to the limit. I thought Dann and I might have to sit on the stairs to eat. The biggest problem is keeping the guests out of the way of my working crew so I posted No Entrance signs on my kitchen door and chased the guests upstairs. Dann had lit a fire in the upstairs bedroom and we put the hors d'oeuvres there. Guests circulated and visited in and out of the five bedrooms while we organized the kitchen.

Next we planned an International Dinner for 32 Homemakers (I plan the menu and send out recipes). A friend who knows me well said, "It's going to be quiet around your house when Tony leaves, but not for long." She was right.

Much to our delight because Christmas fell on the weekend with unused vacation time, Andy got 10 consecutive days and he and Tony drove home for Christmas. The whole family gathered for the first time in 10 years.

Our exercise class has just had our annual treadmill stress test. All of us have slipped a bit in our performance and so the powers-that-be have increased the intensity of our exercise and added five minutes. Tacking five on to 45 is awful. As I was one of the last ones to do the test, the trend was obvious and my buddies gave me pep talks on running to the last drop to get the class average up, but I'm no martyr. When I'm exhausted I quit with no class spirit. We've completed three years and the good doctor has applied for more grants to extend the program. I enjoy those mornings when I don't have to go.

Going north to the cottage over one weekend in search of snow we found it so deep that we couldn't go outside without either cross-country skis or snowshoes. We got more snow than we could cope with during one day of winter training class at the

Arboretum. That long winding drive crosses the prairie and nobody else wanted to drive so Dann put the truck into four wheel drive for me and switched cars. The drive had not been plowed and the snow was deep. All the cars trying to park in the unplowed lot created pandemonium. Also we found no speaker. He had come, but decided we must have cancelled and left, getting stuck on his way out. They sent me back with the truck to look for him. We pushed him back on the road and persuaded him to return. My passengers had a stimulating ride as I could hear them inhale every time I gunned it through the deep snow There were only two wheel tracks (on this two-way road), so every time I met an oncoming car coming in for class, I would swing out into new snow which worried my two riders. I found it exhilarating to drive a car that performs so beautifully under such difficult situations. My exhilaration was taken down at supper that night when Mike said, "Just remember, Mom, that when a four wheel drive gets stuck it is much harder to get it out.

Fran, after your digs about such long waits I sat down and wrote this whole letter in one day and wished it happy flying.

CHAPTER 10

It's A Girl

OCTOBER 22, 1983

Dear Cousins,

This is the third generation that has waited expectantly. The Willetts have finally struck gold with a girl, but you need to hear the fish story from the beginning. Although we went fishing in Canada again last June with Georgiana and Bob we changed our location. Instead of being flown in and dropped at a tent site, they flew us in to a fishing lodge. We lived in luxury with showers, a flush toilet, and a refrigerator, but not many fish. We've decided we have to choose between luxuries or an abundance of hungry fish, but this also meant we were more reachable than when we are in a wilderness site. On the last night when we came in after the evening fishing, the lodge notified us of a phone call. We connected quickly with Jason in Minneapolis who announced, "We have a keeper and it's a girl." A girl in this family is a novelty as that is something that neither Jay's grandfather, his father nor his brothers have produced.

Jay is one that has not followed a single career path as he has gone from computers with IBM to recycling and environmental concerns and to Finance Manager for the Metropolitan Council of St. Paul. His loyalties have been divided between Wisconsin and Minnesota.

46

Thus began a busy summer. As it was sixty years ago that Dann's father and his older brothers built the cottage on Lake Nebagamon, this year we held a 60th birthday party that has been in the planning for two years. Fifty-three Willetts came that weekend. A few slept in the beds in the cottage, we slept in our Scamper camper on the truck, a few rented mobile homes and the rest slept, or tried to, in tents. Most of our family came except for Andy who had a college reunion. Tony was there and even six week-old baby Allison, who slept in a tent. I had decorated a 14" round cake drawing a sketch of the cottage in the frosting on the top. I made it a week in advance. It's a worry transporting 325 miles in August heat without damage, expecting one's frosting not to crack is optimistic but I was prepared by carrying all the colors of leftover frosting for necessary repairs. I put my Willett genealogy notes in order and created a set of nine family trees on placemat size paper—230 years and nine generations of Willetts and gifted each family with a set.

After that exciting weekend "Grandpa Dann" and I took the two little boys home with us. Their parents and Tim left for a week of backpacking in the Porcupines. We did not offer to take six week-old Allison.

In September we put the Scamper back on the truck and headed west spending the first weekend with Andy in North Dakota. His terrible schedule required getting up at 3:30 a.m. seven days a week to check the drills on his oil fields, and driving back to his office to phone a report to Houston by 8:00 a.m. He has hired a live-in babysitter to take over when he's called away. We drove from there to Glacier National Park. Because it was past tourist season, we didn't worry about finding a camping site, but did get a lot of temperature variance. It had been so hot when we left home that we slept on top of our sleeping bags. As we moved west we crawled inside the bags, then we switched to warmer, down bags. At the next stop we took the summer bags back out and spread them on top of the winter ones and finally after it snowed all night we resorted to motels. After Glacier we drove to Washington and visited Lisa, who was our foster daughter 20 years ago. She, with husband and 13 year-old daughter, Jenny, live on 20 wooded acres where they are building a 2 ½ story log cabin. Lisa and I talked non-stop for two days while we canned tomatoes and pears. She repeatedly expressed appreciation for all that we had done for her the three years that she lived with us, but I disclaimed, "We didn't do much Lisa. We simply opened doors so that you could see what opportunities awaited you if you worked at it." Dann climbed to the roof and helped Rick with construction problems and I entertained Jenny with stories about her mother when she was her age. Coming back we camped in the North Dakota badlands and did all the scenic drives and self-guided walks. The last weekend we spent in Minneapolis with Jason and played with that new baby granddaughter.

Coming home we found Mike in the process of buying an 1854 farmhouse, eight miles from us. It has stood vacant for a long time and been vandalized. Someone had attempted an addition to the house, but either stopped in the middle of every project or did it wrong so Mike has his work laid out for years to come. The passive solar on the south wall leaked and had to be re-done, the circular staircase goes from second floor to first, but from first to the basement one chooses between jumping or dropping. The beautiful barn siding on the outside was installed horizontally instead of vertically so every time it rains the water gets behind and inside; the furnace had to be replaced; the well pump wouldn't run and the water tested unsafe; the old well had to be filled with cement. Susan and I tried to clean. It had been vacant so long it looked like a haunted house of cobwebs. With the cathedral ceiling, plus rafters and beams most of that cleaning had to be done over our heads.

Mike and Sue drafted a moving crew of four pickup trucks with 13 adults and six preschoolers who were constantly in front of whatever came through. My job was to feed the crew at noon. As the kitchen wasn't yet done, I operated with crock pots and warming trays and served stew and sourdough cinnamon rolls. When we called the next morning we discovered the whole family was freezing and sick. Although the new furnace was working, this drafty old farmhouse with no storm windows was leaking heat like a sieve. We drove out with a hot supper and a "housewarming" present—a box of matches and firewood for the first fire in their first fireplace. Mike bought quantities of plastic and stapled it over the leaky solar, the windows and the open stairway hole. How awful to be sick in an unfamiliar place that is uncomfortably cold. Our fire and hot supper lifted their spirits. We offered a couple of temporary bedrooms, but they refused. Mike said they had to get the kinks out of the system and couldn't do it from elsewhere. Lucas acted like an ornery three-year-old when they took him back to the old apartment to finish cleaning. The new tenants had started to move in and Luke put one foot over the threshold of his old bedroom and said, "This is MY bedroom. What is all that stuff doing in here?"

After helping Mike with his problems, we returned home to a call from Andy saying that he is being transferred back to Denver. I asked dutifully if he needed to ship Tony back to us, but he thinks he can handle it this time. This is a good move for him. We had wondered how long he could last on the terrible work schedule he was maintaining. He had been home only six hours the preceding week and he worries that's no way to raise a small, unusually active boy.

Our most devastating news is that our five-month-old granddaughter has a hole in her ventricle wall that requires heart surgery. Her heart is working at three times the normal rate. The doctors put her on medication trying to slow her heart down so that she could gain some weight. She gained a bit. They will stall up to one year as they'd like to get her weight up and want her to be a little older but that hole must be closed. The chances for success in this operation are high, but what a stressful year for Jason's family.

After watching the agonies of my family moving I have decided I want no part of this. When the time comes I think it would be nice if Dann and I died simultaneously—in bed—in our present home.

February 14, 1984

Dear Cousins,

We have a new lease on life after taking a long weekend up north at our "summer" cabin. We took snowshoes and cross country skis. The snow depth of 30 inches created a few problems. One needs snowshoes to go anywhere outside, even to the outdoor privy so we learned to start well in advance. We snowshoed in the back swamp, but the snow depth makes it tiring. We hated to waste beautiful daylight hours indoors, but found it necessary to spend a lot of time resting with our feet up on the old wood stove. We limited slugging through that deep snow to two hours. We also did night skiing on the frozen lake where the snow depth was more manageable and the terrain flat with no hills. The full moon reflecting off the snow provided ample light. It pleased me to get away from the phone and daily troubles.

Coming home through Minneapolis we checked on our littlest Willett. What a thrill to see her smile—something we went without for six months. The effort to postpone the necessary surgery until she was bigger failed as her weight just wouldn't surpass 10 pounds so a week before Christmas they performed open heart bypass surgery. It was fortunate that they didn't wait any longer as her heart was pumping so hard it was already damaging to the valve, enlarging the heart and causing pulmonary pressure. Following surgery she was on a respirator, had four IV"s, two chest drains, catheter, heart and blood pressure monitors. They administered curare for 12 hours to paralyze her so that she wouldn't fight the tubes. Her father said she looked like something in the TV soaps. Once they removed the tubes, she recovered with lightning speed. We are hopeful that they succeeded in completely closing the hole. I hung her snapshot on our tree as that was the best Christmas present we received.

Dann and I decided the only way I was going to find time to play my new organ was if I was forced to do it so for Christmas he gave me organ lessons, but it's still hard to set aside daily practice time.

Georgiana and Bob visited for the weekend. We didn't mean to provide such unusual excitement. When they arrived Dann was in the basement working with his power saw. I called down to announce their arrival, but wanting to finish what he was working on, he shoved through one last board. Dann is usually very careful, but he came tearing upstairs sure that he had lost his finger. I wrapped a cloth around it and clamped his other hand over that to control the bleeding. We abandoned our guests and took off for the emergency room. This delayed supper, but the doctor saved the finger. If one has to do this sort of thing with company present, Georgiana and Bob are at the top of my list for the proper guests. They answered our phone, made coffee, started supper and mopped up the bloody kitchen floor. Fortunately the tendons were not cut. If Dann continues to exercise it diligently for the next year he should regain all motion. He got tired answering questions about what had happened, plus he must have been embarrassed to admit that he had been careless, so he developed a stupendous story about going to Disney World and struggling with an alligator. One day when telling this story to a lady in the office, with no hesitation she asked, "Would you like to hear about the three elephants that sat on my hand and squashed it?"

It hasn't been monotonous in Dann's office either. One day I was there alone, as I often am, and a strange man strode in from the street. He stood in front of my desk screaming that I was a whore and should go back to Milwaukee where I belonged and he spit all over my papers. Obviously this man had a thing against women. I usually take the dog with me to the office because on some days I keep large amounts of cash. I called Ranger, curled up in the corner, and he came bounding up ready to play. Grabbing his collar I held him tight. Startled, the man looked at the dog and left while I called the police. I could have used more unfriendliness on Ranger's part, but it turned the trick. There are a lot of strange people out there walking the streets.

APRIL 6, 1984

Dear Cousins,

    I'm glad you all enjoyed my English journal. I didn't think people would be interested. You make me feel guilty for not writing more. I've always wanted to write and I can't find the time. I have a friend who solved that problem by getting up at 6:00 a.m. and did her writing before the world woke up. I am already up by then but doing something else.

    Fran, you wondered if any of us got the flu...yes. And to make matters worse Dann's turned into pneumonia. Both of us were sick at the same time and it dragged on for two months. We alternately struggled to get up so one of us could open the office. When we thought we were over the flu we flew to EPCOT Center and had two great days before we got ill again. We did enjoy those two days, but next time I would like President Reagan to plan his schedule differently. That army of security agents scurrying around interfered with everything. The young gals in blue jeans and T-shirts looked about college age and were hard to identify until they stopped us from moving in close.

    We are now 3 ½ years into our exercise research class and they have applied for a grant extension. I don't want to continue and I don't want to stop. I can't win, can I or is it that I can't lose?

    I finally resorted to reading this missile in the bathtub as I was desperate for unscheduled time. I have posted a note on the back door that says "NO, I can't." Dann inquired what that meant and I said that's to remind me what to say when anybody asks me to do anything.

We certainly are all different. Dorothy, I don't know how you can possibly write letters at 4:30 a.m. that make sense.

According to Georgiana's figuring this bird has been traveling since 1943. I can't believe that I was in it in then as I would have still been in high school and don't think you would have wanted me at that flighty age.

CHAPTER 11

Outpost Fishing

MAY 14, 1984

Dear Cousins,

Yes, we did it again. Young Lucas walked around for weeks announcing that he was going to get a baby sister and he was right. Michelle arrived March 1, narrowly missing Leap Year Day. She was born on a Thursday. Her mother has Monday evening classes and didn't miss a class. This meant that Grandpa and Grandma were babysitting with a four day-old "nursing" child.

When visiting with Fran and Al, the stories she told about our Grandfather Elijah Tracy and his Civil War experiences kept us spellbound. They took us to meet Cousin Ethel and I peppered her with questions about our family history. She and I have something in common—both of us have a Hibbard parent and a William's parent. When I searched family records I learned that her Hibbard grandfather George was brother to Elijah, my Hibbard grandfather. In addition her father Will Williams was a brother to my other grandfather, Charles Williams. She shifted stories so rapidly between this grandfather and that grandfather without clarifying which was which that Dann quietly gave up, picked up the Reader's Digest and silently retreated to the corner.

It appears that my osteoporosis research project may go down the drain. The Federal government turned down the doctor's request for additional funds, but he's continuing the program for one more year at our cost. He told us that the normal drop in bone minerals for women over 35 would be 10%. In our controlled group he shows a 1% drop for the entire four years.

I have a class of rambunctious fifth graders waiting for me to take them through the School Forest this morning so must dash...

OCTOBER 21, 1984

Dear Cousins,

This is the darnest bunch of "birds"—not one of us seems to stay home long enough to write letters. I always re-read my last letter and am amazed to see that so much has happened since I last wrote.

Our fishing trip with Georgiana and Bob took a different direction this year. They flew us a hundred miles in to an outpost camp. The owner must have worried about having two women out in the wild so they dropped us at one of the few cabin sites. He shouldn't worry about women. He should worry about the beer drinking men who preceded us and left the place filthy. We struggled through two hours of scrubbing before we considered it habitable. We were alone on that beautiful, quiet lake, but in the middle of the week the plane flew in to move us to another site. By this time we didn't want to move and maybe have to clean up another site. The plane landed during our fresh fish dinner and the next party was aboard leaving us no choice. The pilot had worried about us (because we had complained) and now he promised to fly us out every night to a motel if we didn't like this new tent site. We were flown another hundred miles to a tent outpost. Dann and I fell in love with this site that perched on a huge rock sheltered by a few trees with a narrow rocky point jutting out into the lake The site boasted two inadequate motorboats. Georgiana and Bob were uneasy in a tent site, but we assured them that to have three walls and a tarp over the potty was a luxury, and that it didn't matter that it was see-through plastic. We declared the dining tarp would be a gold mine if we got pelted with wind or rain and it didn't matter if the pressure wasn't holding on the Coleman stove because we had a neat outdoor cooking setup—a six-foot tripod with hanging hook under a tarp also full of holes. We had flown far north. With summer solstice approaching, daylight still lingered at 10:00 p.m. and by 5:00 a.m. streaks of crimson and pale pink were stretching across the sky. When Dann and I got up for our night call we often walked out onto the rocky point to admire the gorgeous full moon. It felt strange being alone on the lake and realizing that if you aren't making any noise there won't be any.

We did have a serious problem. We took out both motorboats the last afternoon because we planned to fish a distance away from camp. On the trip heading back to camp we broke a few rules—like not crossing the other boat's wake except at 90 degrees and not wearing life preservers. Georgianna and Bob were ahead of us when Dann, worrying about the possibility of big boulders just under the surface, changed direction and this angled us across the wake of the other boat. Water swished over our freeboard and tipped us onto one side throwing Dann out. Because we had been worrying about submerged, invisible rocks, I had been lying across the prow hanging on to both gunwales as I searched for lurking obstacles. This probably kept me in the boat. Georgiana and Bob did not notice, went around a bend in the river and puttered along home. In all the years we've been doing this, I have never run the motor. It terrified me to suddenly find myself alone in a motorboat with no idea how to stop it. The incoming water had filled much of the boat making it impossible to move back to the motor as every time I moved the boat would tilt and stringers of fish would swish around me. Dann was okay and swimming. Before he flew into the air he had unconsciously shifted the gears, which throttled the speed to half, so I was making drunken circles around him. Both of us worried about him getting close to the motor that I was not controlling. He finally managed to swim between my drunken circles and reached the bow of the boat. Holding his feet straight down this acts as an anchor and it steadied the boat while he instructed me what to do. I stopped the motor and bailed what I could. We decided to paddle toward shore as I couldn't lift Dann back into the boat. It was tough going because, in my ignorance, I had shifted into reverse and I was paddling against the motor. Before long, his feet touched one of those invisible, big boulders. Stepping up on it brought the water level down to his waist and enabled him to easily step back into the boat. As the duffle bag was still dry I helped him to strip and put on dry clothes. We bailed some with the minnow bucket, restarted the motor and went home. Arriving at camp we told our story, laid the gear out to dry and Dann took me right back out for a lesson on how to start, stop and steer. We have a long list of things that we were thankful for that afternoon.

It's hard to keep track of our expanding family. Andy is still getting sent out to the oilfields for two weeks at a crack and manages with a live-in babysitter. Jason bought a dilapidated old farm southeast of St. Paul, surrounded by 13 beautiful acres. The house is in awful shape so Tim hired out to him for a month, remodeling for his brother. Dann went along occasionally as Mr. Fix-it just can't keep away from reconstruction work. Mike has opened a body shop this summer. It's in Verona, a few miles south of Madison and they are already booking six weeks in advance.

In September we drove around Lake Superior in our camper recuperating from our busy summer. In our spare time we are attempting to figure out how to retire as we realize there are many things we'd like to do. My exciting news is that Dann and I will be leaving next month for the National Realtors Convention in Honolulu. I know this is old hat to many of you, but it is one place we thought we'd never get to. Dann tells everybody he is taking his secretary.

CHAPTER 12

Flying Into the Sun

FEBRUARY 19, 1985

Dear Cousins,

Ede, have you seen that newspaper article from the New York Times that Grandpa Elijah wrote about his Civil War experiences? His words drew vivid pictures of him and a fellow soldier trudging through the mountains as they tried to get from the hospital in Indiana back to their unit in Chattanooga. His breakfast description of cold coffee and raw bacon consumed in pouring rain gives me shudders.

Hawaii was breathtaking. I attended some convention classes and outings for spouses, although I really wanted to do Christmas shopping. I participated in a class of hula dancing on the lawn of the Hilton Hawaiian Village and we attracted many passers-by. I attended a session on Wok cooking, a house and garden tour, Hawaiian history in costume, the Honolulu Boy's Choir and together Dann and I toured the Arizona Memorial. A VIP (volunteer-in-place) described where he was on that fateful morning. As he spoke, the confusion, pandemonium and terror transported us right back to that historic day. The last day we squeezed in a dinner cruise off Waikiki Beach, a poor choice. I had been controlling a headache all day with aspirin, but we didn't want to forfeit our free tickets and boarded even though the seas were rolling. Belatedly I took Dramamine. Preceding dinner they served some mild and delicious fruit drinks. When the band played dreamy dance music, we couldn't resist that either. Lesson learned: aspirin, Dramamine, what must have been rum punch, rolling seas, and dancing do not make an acceptable combination.

We flew from Oahu to Kauai. We're getting addicted to Bed & Breakfasts. Our hostess on Kauai was a gourmet cook who had worked as chef worldwide. Surprises appeared daily on the breakfast table. We suggested she skip the last day as we were leaving early, so she offered supper instead: fresh mahi mahi, Portuguese potato salad, a melt-in-your-mouth apple dessert and her best German wine. She cooked and served in a long dress with bare feet peeking out underneath. We flew by helicopter over the mountainous center of Kauai which doesn't work for me on an empty stomach so we corrected that by sampling poi. I try everything, but in retrospect I would have preferred an upset stomach.

On the Big Island we stayed within the national park at the Volcano House, right on the rim of the crater. When we registered they asked if we wanted to be awakened if Mauna Kea started to blow as the seismographs were showing activity, but sadly we got no call and slept peacefully. Hiking 11 miles over the 1974 lava fields, we climbed over and around black rocks of all sizes and formations as far as the eye could see. We found this awesome and didn't see another soul all day. It is important that one stay on the trails, but that's a lot harder than following trails in the School Forest as these are marked only by piles of rock. Next time we'll know that when hiking for hours in the hot wind one should always carry water.

July 24, 1985

Dear Cousins,

Sorry this is late. Georgiana passed it to me while we were on our annual Canadian fishing trip and you can't expect me to write while we're fishing. We went back to the Broken Jaw site again this year and this time our difficulties occurred when we tried to come home. The plane stopped to check on us toward the end of the week.

The pilot suggested a Friday pick-up because of approaching bad weather. Dann said, "No way. I want my whole week."

"OK, but I'll pick you up first thing Saturday morning," the pilot replied. We got up early Saturday, quickly packed our gear and waited. Fog drifted here and there leaving only a narrow channel of visibility above the tree line. And we waited. We couldn't go fishing. We couldn't eat because the supplies were packed. We couldn't even stay warm. And we waited. Around noon we heard the low hum of the Beaver as it skimmed over the treetops, landed on the water and taxied up to our rock. I am allotted the seat next to the pilot because of my queasy stomach. Even getting prime seating I suffered through a rough ride. The pilot followed the waterways all the way out in case he had to set down. Low clouds forced him to fly low and he kept his map spread out on his lap. When we scooted across the lake at home base he commented, "Whew! That's the last flight for the day." As he did not pick us up as early as we had been expecting him, I inquired how many pickups he had made before ours and he replied, "You were the first and the last. I had to put down three times before I reached your camp because of poor visibility."

When I asked how many were still waiting for a pick-up that wasn't going to materialize he said, "Five."

The following month was our cottage week. Four friends joined us. Both of the two women were naturalists, whom I had worked with in the School Forest and we spent lots of time "slurping" around in the swamp or out on the sand barrens. We spotted a pair of foxes, a few deer, a skunk, and a pair of nesting eagles. At night Dann continually called in the barred owls, which were numerous and vocal, and he spent his days taking our male guests sailing.

Our big excitement is that we've purchased an IBM PC for the office. This is supposed to simplify the bookwork so that I can retire to part-time. As I was completely computer illiterate, for weeks I had to double my time just to survive. I feared that probably one can't teach an old dog new tricks, but did find it challenging and stimulating. Why, for instance, when you want to close down and stop do you have to press the start button? Jason's wife spent a lot of time teaching me. In return we suggested that they go out overnight and let us baby-sit. Unfortunately Allison had picked up a cold and she experienced great difficulty breathing. Grandpa Dann and I were up with her seven times during that overnight and worried most of the night. That brought back memories.

OCTOBER 25, 1985

Dear Cousins,

Yes, I have finally mailed the Hibbard genealogy placemats that I had promised. Good old Murphy's Law kicked in. Every problem that I could have, I did. I sorted all the corrections and additions that you sent me including the summer crop of babies. We had a problem with the ink running and it took a while before I was satisfied with the lamination and then I couldn't find mailers large enough. I got peppered with questions from the laminators when I picked the placemats up as they had read them in great detail and wondered if I did this professionally. I hope you are all as pleased with them as I am, and that you didn't get as frustrated as I did with the delay.

We're expanding again as Andy has re-married. Dann and I drove to Denver in our Scamper for the wedding and stayed afterwards to camp in the mountains. The rest of the family flew in for a long weekend. Andy's house exploded with guests putting floor space at a premium. I can only describe that wedding as memorable. The night before the wedding, inches of wet, sloppy snow dropped on Denver and did not get plowed. Many guests couldn't make it to the church. The bride's mother arrived at the last minute. After the ceremony Tony tore down the aisle, threw his arms around Kate and hollered "Mommy" creating a real tear jerker. Following the service, the bride gently lifted her wedding dress and removed her dress shoes replacing them with tennis shoes. Wet snow on the lines took out the power in Boulder, where the wedding took place. The Holiday Inn, hosting the reception, lost all power from noon until 6:00. When we called to check, they requested that we borrow all the church candles that we could find. This is the first family wedding where the boys haven't made mischief for their brother, but when I mentioned this afterward one said, "Good Heavens Mom, we were having enough trouble just trying to survive the day without creating more problems." The reception took place in inside rooms and Jason spent an hour in the semi-darkness frantically lighting candles. The bride and groom departed for a cabin in the mountains for their honeymoon and fished in spite of the snow. We kept Tony.

I have had such bad back pains that I could hardly walk. The doctor gave me muscle relaxants and sent me to bed for two weeks. It was mental agony to lie there and do nothing and physical agony if I didn't. I inquired of the doctor what I had done to provoke this. His discouraging answer was that I had been too much on the go and under continual stress. In other words don't rush around so much, but how does one slow down? The answer, of course, is that I haven't. We're leaving soon for two weeks in Florida and will be picking up a sailboat that we bought over the phone from friends. Hope we don't run into another blizzard.

January 22, 1986

Dear Cousins,

I started this day at 6:00 a.m. getting up for the osteoporosis exercise class. Next I tore downtown to Vocational School for a class in computing that I am taking along with Dann and Tim. I then worked in the office until noon when I took off for Van Hise School to take a class of 3rd graders to the School Forest for winter tracking. The deep snow supports you for about three steps before you crash through. A day like this is good for my diet—not only did breakfast not get programmed, but lunch was on the run too.

Ede, thanks for worrying about my back, but I don't think that "hanging by one's neck" will help.

Our luck didn't hold for our quick trip south to pick up the sailboat. Going down we chose the scenic way along the Mississippi River. We had planned to camp on the Gulf coast but realized, while still 100 miles away that Hurricane Juan was occupying the campsites we were headed for. Changing course we crossed over to the interior of Georgia. Dropping down on the last day into the Florida panhandle we managed to use our tent for only one night. The state park we chose jutted out into the gulf and had been evacuated and reopened the day before. As we put up the tent in the dark we didn't realize much of it was still under water until we tried to pound in tent stakes. Fortunately the tent was on a raised hummock, but the wind and waves pounded all night.

Hope, we so rarely get to see you that including you in this trip was special.

We had tried to go early enough in the season to avoid winter driving while pulling that boat home and did fine until we crossed the Illinois/Wisconsin border. It was November 10, but we hit the first storm of the year and soon passed cars in the ditch. As we slowly approached home we worried about whether we could pull that boat up our long driveway. Halfway would block the driveway and be worse than nothing. Dann walked the drive first and then gambled that he could do it and he did, but if we had been a couple hours later that storm would have stopped us. We'll moor the sailboat on Lake Mendota next summer and I must learn how to sail as I don't approve of people going out on boats they don't know how to stop.

Did I mention that Dr. Smith received an additional grant of half a million dollars last year? This attaches to the six years we've done and restarts our osteoporosis study. He claims that this is the most extensive study of osteoporosis worldwide. We still have 80 of the original women and 80 more will be added. I have done only minor complaining when I had to arise at 6:00 a.m. and jog and dance around the gym, but I may be doing a lot more griping with the new tests. He now requires a monthly blood test and a 24-hour urine collection. I'm going to let you imagine the irksome difficulty that poses when they do mean 24-hour collection. If we start at 6:00 a.m. on the day of collection, which we all do because we have to get up then in order to make exercise class, then we must get up at 6:00 a.m. the following day even though it's probably Saturday. They cannot cope with 23 or 25 hour collections. In order to run that test they need all the collagen removed from our diet so that it doesn't cover up what they're looking for. This means for two days prior—no meat, poultry, fish, or horse's hooves (which are present in Jell-O). For the blood test we can't eat anything for 12 hours prior. The date for the first collection covered a Scottish banquet so they set a special date for me. The next collection will coincide with a winter weekend at the cottage up north. Traveling with a gallon bottle, a no-meat diet and using an outdoor john sounds like a real blast. Our Dr. Smith is excited about all this and we think he is doing great things—if we all survive.

CHAPTER 13

Traveling Like a Turtle

MARCH 23, 1986

Dear Cousins,

    We're getting better at this grandparent business. This time we produced a double header. Jason notified us that Trevor Thomas arrived February 8, so Allison now has a brother. A few weeks later Andy called from Denver to say that Tony now has a sister—Alessandra Danielle born March 6. We drove to Minneapolis to inspect Trevor and plan on flying to Denver shortly to check on Alex.

    Tim, with his buddies, traveled north for a weekend. We kept the children of Tim's friend Bobbie—ages eight and twelve. I wasn't sure I still remembered what to do with that age, but I think we passed the course. The first night we made pizzas from a kit. The next day we swam at the YMCA and I announced that if either of them wanted to knead part of my bread they could keep it to take home. The second day we traded children with Mike and Sue. We kept two-year-old Michelle. They kept Luke and adding our young guests they took all three to watch the lambing at the farm next door to them. The kids even rode horseback. I don't know what we'll do next time—it looks like they did everything this weekend.

    On February 1, Dann took that first step toward retirement. He turned over our property management to Tim, only now Dann seems busier than ever. He found two lots that were such a good buy he couldn't resist and he plans on building a house this summer for resale purposes. What kind of retirement is that? In response to that I explained to him that I am developing a ten-year plan. I want to sail a lot with our new boat, enroll in computer and organ classes, camp and canoe often, do more Scottish country dancing, travel—specifically Nova Scotia, Scotland, Australia, the Bahamas, & Mexico. The rest of the time I want to play with grandchildren. Now I'm off to bed. It's been a strenuous weekend being a pseudo-grandmother.

I AM taking it easy, Ede and Fran. We have a tenant who has trouble paying her rent so she cleans for me to whittle down her debt. What a luxury.

July 25, 1986

Dear Cousins,

Tony, who is now eight, flew in from Denver. We picked up his six-year-old cousin Luke and took both boys north with us for our cottage week. I belong to the school of thought that it's better to have two boys than one. In the middle of the week the rest of Mike's family joined us and then Jason's family arrived bringing our people count to 12. Constant rainy weather promoted much visiting. It was supposed to be a restful week, but I only rested afterwards. Kids falling out of bed every night or walking in their sleep interfered with my sleep.

This semi-retirement is not working. We haven't even found time to moor the sailboat on Lake Mendota. That was supposed to be #1 priority for the summer.

What keeps us busiest is planning a Willett reunion. One hundred years ago Dann's grandfather sailed into New York harbor. This seemed an appropriate year to gather his descendants. George Henry had 11 children and as we are including descendants of his brothers and sisters, this project grows like a downhill snowball. Acceptances are coming in from California, New York and Georgia creating a golden opportunity for an amateur genealogist like me.

Also we're getting ready for a three-week trip to Nova Scotia with our Scamper camper. This is our "me" vacation, the one thing this year for just Dann and me. We're ready for a little solitude. In the Scamper we travel with the world on our backs like a turtle. When at home, we park the unit next to the garden. When we're ready to roll, Dann carefully backs the Ford truck underneath and fastens the Scamper onto the truck bed. The living quarters fill the bed of the truck, but they fold down when we're on the road. When we stop at night after a hard day of driving, springing the top is like snapping up a card table. We have a double bed over the cab and yes, it takes a little climbing to go to bed. This beats setting up a tent for people who think they are semi-retired

OCTOBER 23, 1986

Dear Cousins,

As we traveled through Nova Scotia we took Wisconsin's rainy weather along with us. Camping along a big body of water the first night, condensation leaked through one of the ceiling cracks—probably snow damage we hadn't noticed earlier. I asked Dann, "If it leaked that much with just dew what will it do if it rains?" Then it poured non-stop for three days. As we still had weeks to travel, Dann decided this had to be fixed and thought he could do it with tar. We were deep into Quebec and having language difficulties. Dann's World War II-French proved inadequate. He rolled words off like a pro. The "merci bonjour" got us into immediate trouble because he would get an unintelligible response until his "juno comprende vous" would stop the flow of French. I never did figure out where he learned the "I love you", but that didn't help either. It was hard driving on mountainous roads with dishpans in the camper positioned under numerous leaks. Unfortunately they wouldn't stay positioned. We found a dictionary, Dann memorized the word for tar and we hit the hardware stores, but apparently he was getting the accent on the wrong syllable. He resorted to drawing pictures of rain dripping through the camper roof. Something finally registered and the clerk said, "Ah, plasteeck ceement". Standing on a picnic table Dann stretched to his limit to reach and caulk all the seams, but this worked.

In Montreal we walked through the old town section and sampled Escargots at a sidewalk café. I didn't realize what a large city Montreal is until we tried to leave it and could not. Somehow we had to find a way up on any one of the three bridges that take you off the island and we couldn't find the access to any, traffic was bad, it poured continually and when we stopped to ask for directions no-one spoke English. We finally succeeded when we realized that EST is east and Quest is west. It was still storming as we drove along the highway on the south shore of the St. Lawrence which catapulted the waves over the highway. Reaching Glace Bay, in Nova Scotia, we found some third cousins of Dann's, who not only insisted we stay with them, but wanted us to stay for a week because, they moaned, relatives never come way up here. We explored an old slope coal mine under the ocean where Dann's ancestor had worked as a miner. It extends out 10 miles, but we didn't go far. We often couldn't stand up as we were surrounded by shored ceilings, dripping water and cold dampness and this gets tedious. Reversely we enjoyed the Cabot Trail much more. The breathtaking scenery counterbalances the high altitude, but the highway goes up and down so rapidly that it gets scary when you think your brakes might be faltering. We visited restored, remote fishing villages and crossed over to New Brunswick on the 5:00 a.m. ferry. In order to be there early, we parked at 10:00 p.m. the night before at the front of the indicated parking lanes. I put on pajamas and crawled into bed. Awakening at 4:30 a.m., I discovered huge semis hemmed us in on all sides and wished I had not elected to go with pajamas. The privacy was not good. We wanted to watch the sunrise, but fog wafted around us all the way across the bay.

The Bay of Fundy is famous for its high tidal range. When the Saint John River empties into the bay at high tide, its flow reverses causing a series of unusual rapids. The moon and tides were right, the hour was right, the location was right, but it didn't happen. A frustrated group of people gathered as only a few ripples sauntered by.

We had cashed our $50 birthday check and turned it into $140 Canadian dollars. This stretched to nine eating sessions including lots of fresh fish, Rappie pie (Arcadian) and Moussaka (Greek).

Continuing down the scenic Maine coastline we enjoyed Bar Harbor and Roosevelt's Campobello International Park, which is a summer cottage with 18 bedrooms. As we drove home through the U.S. checking up on all our relatives' en route it shocked us to see that our odometer registered 5,800 miles.

CHAPTER 14

History Lessons

November 11 1986

Dear Cousins,

Sandwiched between trips, I worked at the polls. I was chairman, worrisome when one machine jammed five minutes after we opened. Long standing lines increased my stress. I called City Hall. Their maintenance engineer picked up the phone and he talked me through—a major achievement for non-mechanical me, but crucial because it meant we were rolling again in 10 minutes instead of the hour it would have taken someone to reach us. This stretches to a 16-hour workday and I manage okay until I get up the next day.

The Willett reunion blasted off soon after our return from Nova Scotia. We held it at our church because when George Henry (Dann's grandfather) immigrated to Madison 100 years ago he was instrumental in founding that church. We're now on the fifth generation of Willett's. If we count the not-quite-born babies, 100 people attended our 100 party. We hung huge charts on the wall, asked everyone to highlight their name to indicate their presence and encouraged people to figure out their relationship to everyone else. Friday was get-acquainted night; Saturday morning we led a historical tour of Madison places that influenced Willett ancestors. We caravanned blithely through heavy traffic to old houses, to Science Hall on campus where George Henry worked in the anatomy lab, to Century House where they had lived, and to Owen Conservation Park that Dann's ancestor had helped lay out. All this brought forth so many stories from everyone that after three hours we simply said stop. We had planned a program at the Saturday night banquet where Dann stole the show. He changed his nametag to read Tom Willett (for his great-grandfather). His sizable, snow white beard had been growing since our Canadian fishing trip in June.

He dressed in knickers and a fisherman's cap and, doing a first person presentation, told how life had been in Tackley, England. Simultaneously we ran a few slides of that village and the old Willett house. Those old stone houses often stayed in the same family for centuries. Another Dan Willett present that day remarked that in the dry humor my Dann had used, feelings of restlessness and resentment towards the aristocracy and the Church of England came across clearly. Temporarily Dann transported us all to a different time period.

MARCH 11, 1987

Dear Cousins,

Can you believe that yesterday we marked the 7th anniversary of our exercise class? We saw ourselves on TV twice this fall and a crew from Boston was here filming again. I had another bad bout with my back so my instructor set up three pages of personalized back strengthening exercises to prevent re-occurrences. Now I exercise at home the four days that I don't have class. They called last week to say my cholesterol is creeping up. They thought my doctor should know and are putting together a printout of my blood tests for the last five years for him. They care for us diligently.

This year, instead of having everyone here for Christmas, we ended up with three Christmases. The Madison families came here for brunch the Sunday before; we flew to Denver the day of Christmas Eve and to Minneapolis over New Year's weekend. The flight to Denver, to be with Andy's family came with surprises when Madison fogged in. The plane, coming from Green Bay, tried twice to land here and then over-passed going direct to Denver. This meant some people who thought they were flying from Green Bay to Madison for Christmas went to Denver instead. Running for a phone we called Andy, "Don't meet our plane because we're not on it. Will call when we arrive." We traveled by bus to Chicago and landed in Denver Christmas Eve, but with luggage lagging far behind. I have decided it's easier to have everybody here.

Are you all aware of Elderhostels? Many are offered all over the USA and in foreign countries. Mostly they're located on college campuses during down time using their teaching staff and dorms. The one we chose was at Jenny Wiley State Park in Kentucky. The lodge had motel-like accommodations with balconies overlooking the woods and lake and a dining room complete with buffet, disastrous for those of us with little self-discipline. We ate each meal with different people. It took about two minutes to find areas of common interest. People came from all walks of life, retired, but finding new ways of making life exciting and we could match stories with the best of them. Most Elderhostels offer three courses and this one taught Dance (mountain, Western Square and clogging), Photography and Local History. The photo class had assignments to turn in pictures for critiquing on the 4th day. Never have I seen so many photographers crawling all over everything. The teacher had encouraged them to get close to their subjects and they did. Every time Dann and I twirled on the dance floor two or three would sneak in close popping flashes. The history class covered the Civil War in eastern Kentucky and we learned about the "War of Northern Aggression." As this was a border state, families sometimes split. We learned about Jenny Wiley, a pioneer woman captured by the Indians who escaped to return home, and about the McCoys and Hatfields because this is their home grounds. Our only free time came from 3:30 until supper at 5:30, so each day after class we would dash off to a hiking trail. We checked our watches, hiked for half of our free time and then reversed wherever we were, so as not to endanger supper. Eastern Kentucky is mountainous and Jenny Wiley State Park nestles in a narrow valley alongside a manmade lake with no level ground. Hiking trails are either up or down. In the time we had we never succeeded in making it to the top of the ridge, but even from halfway up we were awed by the views.

Why don't some of you try an Elderhostel? You'll love it.

APRIL 30, 1987

Dear Cousins,

What an expanding Easter we had! There are now so many of us that we don't fit around our huge dining room table anymore. I relegated the four oldest grandchildren to a card table close by. Andy and family flew in Friday afternoon and Jay and family arrived late that night from Minnesota. The parents of the two little ones swapped stories.

On Saturday we added the Madison families. I experimented with a turkey/broccoli crepe recipe producing them by assembly line. I cooked the crepes, passed to Dann who filled them, passed next to Sue who dribbled the sauce on top. Woe to anybody who asked a question as that destroyed our timing.

After lunch the four brothers left to explore a cave near Mike's house. Mike had asked a local person, familiar with the cave, to take them through. Twenty-five years ago one could ride horseback into that cave but it had silted in over the years so the boys crawled through cold mud for two hours. They crawled back out through the opening covered with shiny, steel gray goop and making a stop at the Verona swimming hole they raced in fully dressed. Then detouring to Mike's house, they stripped and threw everything into the washer, but the clothes still came out slate gray. We all gathered at Mike's house and Tim cooked venison steaks on the outside grills. Later Jay's wife, with all the kids, decorated hard boiled eggs in my kitchen. On Sunday morning she and Andy hid the eggs outside. We limited Luke and Tony to the play yard and Allison and Michelle to the side yard. This stopped the boys from snatching more than their share. Before long we discovered that somehow the eggs had not been completely hard-boiled. The kids collected them carefully in their baskets and I boiled them again for egg salad sandwiches. I enjoyed cooking for that crowd, but had worked on preparation for days. I mixed up my Mom's ham loaf recipe, used Dann's Mother's hot cross bun recipe and experimented with baked potatoes topped with spinach. The weather turned so hot by Sunday afternoon that we moved to the Verona swimming beach and most of the adults and all the kids braved the ice cold water. Imagine swimming on Easter Sunday. After putting the kids to bed, their parents went bowling while Dann and I continued to practice grandparent babysitting.

Monday we arose at 5:00 a.m., laid out breakfast and drove Andy's crew to the airport. Tony was back in school in Denver that same morning only half an hour late. We ate a leisurely second breakfast with Jay's family and a third breakfast with Tim when he stopped for a "business conference" with his boss. Jay stayed another day and we babysat Allison again that evening. When her parents came home she inquired, "Don't you have some place to go again tomorrow? Grandma and I still have things to do."

I can't think of any better entertainment than enjoying the family we have created. It's gratifying to see their enjoyment of each other.

JUNE 21, 1987

Dear Cousins,

I have a horrible story to relate this time around. Tim planned a canoe trip to the Minnesota boundary waters taking his friend Terry, Terry's younger brother and Bobbie's son (aged 15). They launched the canoes on Sunday morning and enjoyed several days of canoeing, but on Wednesday night, Terry, only 40 years old, complained of excruciating pain. Tim did not know at the time that Terry was having a heart attack, but he did know that he had to get him out ASAP. As it was evening, Tim elected not to move immediately for fear of getting lost in the darkness. That tough decision made it a long night for all of them. Tim studied the map and decided to head for a lake that allowed motors as some do not. In the early dawn they moved out. Portaging now meant they would carry not only two canoes and gear for four, but also Terry. The Lord must have been watching as starting across the first portage carrying Terry, they met an oncoming party with a motorized canoe. Those strangers immediately turned around, motored back to base and when Tim's group reached the end of the portage a big speedboat was waiting to pick up Terry and his brother. An ambulance waiting at base camp took him to Grand Marais and from there they flew him to Duluth. He has no recollection of how they got him out of the wilderness.

This left Tim in the hinterlands with two canoes and lots of gear. I asked him if Clay could paddle rear in a canoe and he answered, "He can now." Tim put only enough gear in Clay's canoe to get the bow down out of the wind. All the rest he loaded into his canoe and they shoved off and went around in circles until Clay learned how to steer. The hospital in Duluth said that Terry was lucky to be alive. Tim's comment was "I don't need any more vacations."

Perhaps this semi-retirement is beginning to work after all. We enjoyed our first trip overseas to England so much, that we're going again, this time heading for Scotland. We'll be overseas for five weeks, but I've been getting ready for a year. I read Scottish history out loud at the supper table each night. The Mormons have a branch library here in Madison which I have been searching for genealogy leads and we've been taking Scottish County Dance lessons for months. This way the trip lasts a lot longer than five weeks.

CHAPTER 15

Laddies and Lassies

November 2, 1987

Dear Cousins,

    I thought thirty-seven days of exploring would cure me of my itchy feet—and it did—for seven days, but as soon as I sat down and read my journal I was ready to go again. We stopped for a week at the International Music Festival in Edinburgh and attended 12 different events from bagpipe competition and Scottish country dancing to symphony concerts. Edinburgh is rightfully called the city of the night. We attended the famous Glenlivit distillery fireworks and symphony concert in the park standing in pouring rain. Fireworks set off from the castle ramparts covered the castle hill. This is an extremely popular event. Two hundred people held seat reservations in the bandstand, a select 12,000 held free standing tickets (of which we were two) in the gardens and the other 200,000 stood outside the fence looking in. We left at 11:30 p.m. just before the concert ended as we wanted to avoid the crush of the 200,000 and needed to reach our bus stop in time to catch the last bus. We waited 45 minutes with a crowd of other unwise tourists until we discovered that last bus wasn't coming, which meant a two-mile walk home in the rain. After hours of dancing and standing, our feet cried out in distress. Unfortunately, having come in to the city center riding the busses for only two days, when we reached a fork in the road we didn't know which way to go. Walking into the University Center we asked for directions from two leather-jacketed, long-haired, single-earring, young men. They were aghast that we were wandering the streets and tried to call a taxi for us, impossible because of the massive crowds, so they reluctantly sent us off in the right direction. We relieved the strain on our weary feet by stopping at everything that was open…sampling tea, scones and even pizza. As thousands of people crowd the streets daily, we thought it strange that the next day we bumped into those same young men, plus two that had waited with us at the non-functioning bus stop. All had worried about us and asked with great concern if we had gotten home okay the night before.

The next night, experiencing lovely weather, we decided to walk home again. Revelers still filled the streets. Before long we went by an ice cream shop, which called out to us, next a small grocery store beckoned and we came out munching an apple turnover, we couldn't bypass the fish and chips and finished off having tea at home at 2:00 a.m.

Our master pass allowed us to travel by train, bus or ferry so we did lots of island hopping. Stopping at the Isle of Skye on the Inner Hebrides, we worked on our Nicol genealogy. Our B & B host happened to be a Nicol historian. We followed him into bogs, slipping over hummocks and narrowly missing sheep dung as he led us to a marble monument inscribed Scorrybreck. This was the ancestral home of the Nicholson chieftains for 800 years, dated 1825, the year that they left the area. He exclaimed delightedly that we were on the home grounds for as far as we could see and he pointed out how strategically placed this area was to defend as we could see in all directions. A lone sentry on the headland facing the sea could cover that also. Grass-covered crumbling building walls lay all over.

From there we ferried to the Outer Hebrides finding barren land and lochs (as far as the eye can see), dotted with sheep and peat bank lines. The peat banks stay in the family for generations. If the peat becomes exhausted the family applies to the village council for a new bank. These villager crofters pay nine pounds per year for the use of the land. The men have been brought up on the moors and cover miles across it quickly with a balance that enables them to move lightly and fast from hummock to hummock.

Ferrying back to the mainland we crossed to the Orkneys. The minute the ferry backed off the pier I was in trouble. No whitecaps, just big swells that the ship gently rolled into. They said this was a good crossing, but preserve me from a bad one. I didn't move for two hours. Pentland Firth separates the Atlantic from the North Sea and the current runs fast through here with whirlpools and eddies around the shore. The tidal bore can be very high with the tide rushing one way for five hours and back for seven. Orkney harbors are delightful little ports with narrow streets just wide enough for a horse to turn around. We found 5,000 year old settlements that had been buried by sand and uncovered recently by a storm. Burial cairns, preserved medieval towns and prehistoric finds from the Bronze Age surrounded us. This place has abundant beautiful seascapes, huge jagged rocks, pounding waves filled with playful seals, high winds and swirling mists, and seagulls calling between the deep bleats of foghorns. I was unable to figure out some way to return without crossing Pentland Firth again, but fortunately for my stomach we had a following wind on our return trip.

We found each island different- on the mystic Isle of Skye, which is part of the Inner Hebrides, we found Nicol ties and a strong Scottish influence. The lonely Outer Hebrides were windswept and non-commercial. The ancient Orkneys took us back to historical times of different climes and cultures. Each was special in its own way.

We spent the last week in Wales and always stayed in B & B's, even enjoying the one where we shared a common wall with a cow. I am addicted to this traveling. It's when I get home that's tough as it takes two weeks before my system stops trying to sleep at the wrong time of day.

Dann has laboriously earned the title of family electrician. My dad taught him well. He helped Tim with the wiring in his building where he is creating an apartment on third floor and then he helped Mike who is remodeling his roof and re-wiring his entire upstairs.

February 25, 1988

Dear Cousins,

    As some of you know, I have always said someday I want to write a book called "Dear Mom" based on my letters to my Mom. Needing a push in this direction, I signed up for a short course on campus in Creative Writing. I couldn't believe that first class. The teacher looked to be about 16 years old. Long dangly earrings swung as she moved and she was so supple that she sat on a straight chair with her legs crossed under her. Everyone looked younger than my kids. She started with poetry, something I can't do and gave out assignments. I procrastinated for 6 ½ days before deciding I had to produce something or not show up again. Remembering that one needs to write about what one knows, I wrote about the night Mom died when I held her hand all that night. I turned my paper in unsigned and shoved it under the pile of manuscripts, but eventually my turn came. When I finished reading aloud the classroom remained silent and then I saw tears streaking down many faces. They said the imagery made them feel that I was only telling part of the story. One said that he really would have liked to know that little old lady. I thought that was funny. She wasn't a little old lady – to me. I decided that if they could say all those good things the first night then I didn't care what bad things they might say thereafter. Although the class went from college freshmen to a grandmother (me), it did what I had wanted it to do. It convinced me that I could write, but the growing pains are tough.

    We have just finished major renovations upstairs. This, too, is part of my long range retirement plan that includes – don't wait to fix up the house until just before you leave. In the early years of living in this big old farm house we moved around the cracked ceilings. This time we emptied three bedrooms. Tim brought the crew and they dry walled. Dann painted and we sanded the beautiful oak floors. Then we shifted back, stashed everything in those three rooms and repeated the process in the other two. This has taken over a month and we have now arrived at the stage of endless lost and found.

Our exercise class held an eight-year celebration breakfast. I can't believe that almost all of us are still doing something that unpleasant for that long.

I'm sorry that you're having dizzy spells, Hope. It's too bad that there isn't some way for you to work part-time. I can't stand it when people tell me to take it easy so I won't tell you that, but I am grateful that I didn't have to work a full-time job after we had kids. I know, I just worked three jobs, each part-time.

CHAPTER 16

Half Retired and Struggling

June 3, 1988

Dear Cousins,

Acquiring a second generation family is easier than the first time around. We've finally learned how to produce girls. Elara Haley, born March 27, was delivered by midwife at home. Counting Elara, this makes three for Jason.

We have retired that wondrous Scamper that attached to the back of our truck, progressed to a little Chinook camper and taken our first trip. It has less storage than the Scamper, but gets better mileage and that's how we set priorities. It took us several days to figure out that everything has to have a place and be in it and everything has to be done in a set order. When one makes one's bed in this Chinook, one lies in it because there is no space left to do anything else. We use the portable potty only at night because during the day that space fills up with sleeping bags. We now have access from the front to the back while in transit, which means that the non-driver can lie down and rest one's paralyzed rear-end whenever necessary. The refrigerator is truly a refrigerator so we don't have to search for ice anymore. We have a furnace and an air conditioner and big windows with screening so that at night it's like sleeping outdoors, but without bugs. I call this togetherness. We traveled 6,000 miles visiting Andy in Denver, Lisa, our foster daughter in Spokane, Washington and Jason in Minneapolis. I told people that we were just checking on our new granddaughter in Minnesota, but took the long way around. We camped in national parks and stopped to see the Redwoods, an archeology site on the desert, floated down the Rogue River with friends, visited Crater Lake in Oregon during a snowstorm and viewed the devastation at Mount St. Helens.

We have a tenant waiting for a leg amputation probably caused by exposure to Agent Orange while fighting in Vietnam. He has been trying to write his memoirs, but I know how depressed he is and wished I could do something for him. In lieu of any better idea, I left a note by his door telling him that I thought he might need cheering up and that I had said a special prayer for him. He wrote back saying my note flabbergasted him. He felt words of thanks were insufficient so he was having a High Mass said in my name and that he knew we had different religions, but thought we had the same God. I was also flabbergasted. I don't quite know what this means, but I got the general drift. I'm glad if I helped.

This semi-retirement is a misnomer. Two "Mr. Fixits" co-exist in my family. Dann and Tim happily roll from one remodeling job to the next. Dann jumped at an opportunity to purchase an old house in Shorewood that had had no tender loving care for generations. Those two guys happily tore it apart. It took a lot of throwing out before they added four feet to the kitchen and remodeled that whole room. They also added a new furnace, aluminum siding and new bathrooms and sold it before they had finished. They had to promise completion by June 15th and that put a crimp in the schedule because part of the crew goes fishing in Canada in early June.

AUGUST 17, 1988

Dear Cousins,

First, let me straighten out that it was Georgiana who arranged for the repair of the Hibbard gravestone foundations. I checked on Mom's stone. It looks great. Both my brothers said that as Georgiana did all the work she shouldn't have to pay for it too and they will do that. Both of our grandparents are there and I find it fascinating that our grandfather Elijah is supposed to have established this cemetery many years ago. American flags for Civil War veterans flutter all over.

I must respond to somebody's comment that her son's landlord was out to get all he could or something to that effect. This is a common attitude every time anyone gets a rent increase. It really bugs me because I don't like to be the bad guy. Most landlords I know try hard to keep expenses down. Don't you think that we should be entitled to get a 10% return on money we have invested and a reasonable salary for the unreasonable hours we put in? We don't even manage that. Many people sell out for this reason and then everyone complains that there is no available housing. Our property taxes and utility bills on these buildings have increased tremendously and the raises we give never equal the cost of living increases. Sorry for the soapbox.

We took ten-year-old Tony and eight-year-old Luke with us to the cottage again this year and we all swam constantly in beastly hot weather. We have a problem in the lake as lice coming off the ducks switch to humans and bite leaving an itch like a mosquito bite. A shower after swimming and brisk toweling helps to counteract this, but a shower causes a problem when we have no indoor plumbing. The best we could do was to pump several pails of water, set them in the sun to warm while we swam and then drench ourselves, but the water was still frigid. The boys objected to this cold dunking until the weekend when Jason arrived with his family. Five-year-old Allison joined the swimmers and the boys immediately quit objecting to the cold shower. They dumped the pails over her head with great glee saying "But Grandma says this is good for you."

We took a flying weekend to Denver for Andy's graduation as he has completed his master's degree in Accounting. We also squeezed in a Scottish Highland Games performance and enjoyed watching all the competitions and dancing, even joining in with a couple set dances. Lines of brilliant kilts flashed in unison all over the field. It was truly a flying trip as we had company here the day before we left and company the night we came back.

January 10, 1989

Dear Cousins,

The book that I was referring to is the one I have always threatened to do—Dear *Mom*. Shortly before Mom died she commented that she never got to read the book I never wrote. Dann commented he wanted to read it too. That shook me up and I decided I had better make time as it might be later than I think. I started Creative Writing short courses at the Senior Center. It's a lot of work, but those copies of my letters to Mom trigger memories and Dann and I have had lots of fun with recall. This is slow work, but now Dann is taking up where Mom left off. He keeps telling me if I really want to do this, and he really does want me to, I had better give up something else. Obviously I need to give up working.

As usual we have one son in turmoil. Although he's been working in financial consulting in St. Paul for ten years he says he's tired of desk sitting all day. Last fall he located and purchased a small weekly newspaper in Seymour, Wisconsin, population 2,700. He looks at this as a great challenge and we agree. When he gave his notice at the office one guy asked, "What the H—do you know about publishing?"

Jay's answer was, "I didn't know anything about financial investments when I came here, but I can learn anything I want to." I believe he's right, but it makes me tired to think about it. He took over the newspaper on January 1, and worked on his old job through January 3. Then he left for Seymour and his family came here temporarily. They stayed for a week and I soon became exhausted. I couldn't find anything. I either put it up where it might be safe or else it walked to who knows where. We visited the Children's Museum, hiked in the Conservation Park up the road, played Spite and Malice and read stories endlessly. Luke and Michelle came daily to play with their cousins. (I can't remember which one of you asked for directions to this strange game. I think it must be a territorial card game because I've never heard of it beyond southern Wisconsin. You'll find written

Dear Cousins

directions at the end of this missile.) One of the kids arrived sick with the flu; two picked it up before they left, and then left it with us. Other than that, their visit was delightful. We enjoyed the kids if they were behaving, and if they weren't I decided it was somebody else's problem. I would come home from exercise class at 8:00 a.m. and find warm muffins waiting for my breakfast. When I worked in the office I would come home to homemade soup. Three kidlets makes a handful and Gramps was a great back-up and diversion. Jay came for the weekend. He has now rented an old, run-down house so we filled both their cars with survival equipment. They will have to exist using an electric fry pan and hotplate, apartment size refrigerator, sleeping bags, card table and folding chairs and we sent enough food to last through their first supper and breakfast. I washed all their clothes, added plastic bags in each car in case they reverted back to throwing up and sent prayers that the first couple days wouldn't be too rough. They cannot buy a house in Seymour until they sell the one in St. Paul. Until then they are essentially camping out in an empty house.

Some of us have suddenly become aware that we have cholesterol concerns so I've been reading a book about high cholesterol complete with recipes. Mike discovered he had a problem too and the next time he stopped he not only borrowed the book, but swiped my bran muffins. We've all altered our menus to eliminate fats and add bran.

Our holiday festivities lasted two months. Fifty-four square dancers came for a potluck sit-down meal and that strains even my house. The following week my Homemakers did a Taste of Wisconsin meal. I planned the menu using only Wisconsin products, passed out recipes and after dinner gave a slide show of 50 state parks. Yes, we've been to all. In private, I called this my disaster party. Only in private, because everyone except me had a ball and I coped over—and over—and over. Only Dann watched me struggling. It started when the 31 pork chops in the oven set off the smoke alarm. I fixed it, but it kept repeating every time I started something else. That high squeal shatters my cool in a hurry. The woman bringing hors d'oeuvres came late and last. The one bringing baked potatoes with low cal topping didn't realize her full responsibility and came with only the topping. This meant I had to come up with 31 baked potatoes fast. At that point I rejoiced the appetizers were late. The guest of honor never arrived. Somebody told me the next morning she had called and said she didn't like driving on the icy roads, had turned around and gone back home. The idea was great, the food, although a trifle delayed, superb and the company entertaining.

My third and last holiday dinner was for the choir and spouses following our last rehearsal. This time I cooked the whole dinner myself so I could count on it all being there.

We had our traditional oyster stew supper by ourselves on Christmas Eve. Christmas Day we went to Tim's, the day after to Mike's and on New Year's they all came here. The best part of the season has to be family togetherness.

We had a special service at church this morning. The Women's Society plan this day and because I am chairman this year I was responsible for it. I secured a young woman from the Madison Campus Ministry. Sometimes we make our lives more worrisome. Our pastor was out-of-town and I had worried, "Where would that put me if the speaker didn't show?" But all went well and she talked about the need to have quiet times to reflect or meditate and that unless we are strong internally we will not be balanced externally. I needed that sermon.

I have also been planning a teacher in-service. Crestwood School is trying to promote "science in their backyard." This pleased me so much that I gave them the whole load of what exactly we could do for them at the School Forest, at the neighborhood park or in their schoolyard or classroom. I expounded on what they could do for themselves in their schoolyard such as phrenology, soil erosion or study of ecological communities. It challenges me to teach someone who is going to teach someone else as I believe the stone I throw into a river makes ripples in all directions.

Officially this is Grandparents Sunday. Unofficially, it's Grandparents Week at our house. We have the two Madison grandchildren for the week while their parents fly to San Francisco for meetings. Luke is home-schooled so I am going to take advantage and squeeze in a big dose of outdoor education.

As they were exposed to the grandchildren that were here last week with the flu, I have my fingers crossed. It would be just my luck to have more kids with that nasty stuff.

We've had awful weather and keep getting freezing rain which has iced up our long driveway. I've announced if it gets any worse I will have to start taking Dramamine.

Enough for now. I have a date tonight that requires me to dress in my Scottish gear and Dann will wear his Nicol full dress kilt.

MAY 23, 1989

Dear Cousins,

I like the saying "it's only when you're over the hill that you start to pick up speed." It seems to me that things should start to get slower and quieter, but not so. If anything, I seem to be getting better at accumulating ideas and projects to do. This is simply my way of saying I'm sorry I kept the robin so long again. I don't know how that happened, things just got out of control.

In answer to your question: No, I am not progressing much on my "proposed" book. I haven't even opened it since your last letter, but I did sign up for a writing course at the Senior Center—this one for "over 60's". This teacher keeps me so busy that Dann is lucky to keep eating. She keeps trying to light a fire under me. I keep thinking that nobody outside our family will be interested in this family stuff so what she provided was a much needed morale boost. One of my assignments is to write about our grandfather, Elijah Tracy. Please help, I need all the anecdotes that any of you can recall. Especially you Fran as you're the oldest. I am especially interested in your story about taking care of our grandparents during the pandemic following World War I.

Mike's and his daughter's birthdays fall close together, I planned a combination birthday supper and made a dirt cake for a centerpiece. The recipe consists of cream cheese, chocolate pudding mix and crushed Oreo cookies carefully layered in a thoroughly scrubbed flowerpot with artificial daisies inserted. I even added an artificial worm from Dann's fishing box. Those broken Oreos looked more real than actual dirt. I announced that I didn't have a birthday cake, so we would just put candles in a flower pot. Giving Mike a big spoon I asked him to start dishing up. Both children watched in horror, but Mike wet his finger, picked up one crumb and smiled. Michelle still doubted so her father filled a spoon and shoveled it into her mouth.

Jason is busy following Murphy's Law with his newspaper venture. They have not been able to sell their house in St. Paul so the survival equipment we sent to tide them over is still all they've got. It's been five months. Jason enjoys writing, but finds that he has to spend all his time selling advertising. The Milwaukee Journal has such a firm hold in the area that he has about decided there is no future for his paper. He faxes material back to his old office which means he's working the equivalent of two jobs. Plus everybody has been continually sick with the flu—first his family, and then his newspaper staff. He finally decided to get out before he dips too far in the red. He is trying to sell the paper to the Milwaukee Journal and the printing part to the printer and will return to St. Paul and do consulting. They are all exhausted. Dann and I have been there frequently to take care of the kids so that both parents can put in much needed time at the shop.

This semi-retirement is working better. Tim is doing a great job managing the office. Dann and I go in on Monday mornings for a conference and then take off the rest of the week – theoretically. As Tim takes Dann's place, the computer is taking mine. That has worked so well that we've gotten a bigger hard drive and the old IBM came home where I keep it busy. We are finding more benefits to this "over sixty" such as Dann's furniture refinishing class at Vocational School—part of our major effort to clean out the basement.

I still spend time working at the School Forest though and had another request for a night hike. I worked with a 5th grade class doing identification in the morning and working on using our senses in the afternoon to prepare them for the night hike. Walking blindfolded trained our feet to feel the compaction of the trail. By the time we started on our evening hike all 12 kids would have followed me anywhere and done anything. They had no fear of the dark and complete trust that I would not get us lost. I had five parents plus my minister that night. He had expressed great interest in what I was doing in the woods in the middle of the night. I attached two kids to each adult, explaining to the children that they would probably have to help their adult because the adults did not have trained feet. I allow two flashlights—one in front (me) and one in the rear, both covered with red paper as a white light would reduce my night vision. As we walked deep into the woods I dropped off each small group spaced along the trail so that they could get the feel of being by themselves and experience listening to the night sounds. My only instruction was "Do NOT leave the trail no matter what" and after ten minutes the adult sweep in the rear swooped them up bringing all back to me at the front of the line. Both adults and kids love this.

Let me spiel about Lyme's disease, which is our foremost daily topic around here this spring. Previously I had heard about it at winter training lectures. Now it has moved out of the classroom into our woods. I have always requested when I'm with kids in the forest that they bring me any wood ticks they find. I let the tick crawl around in my hand and point out that this female is not going to immediately impact your skin because first she has to reduce her body temperature closer to yours. This sometimes takes hours for her to do this so that stops their panic. I point out these wood ticks are not true insects (identified by counting 6 legs). They are arthropods, like spiders (identified by counting eight legs) and after busily counting legs they begin to realize that rarely are they actually finding a tick.

However the tiny deer ticks, which cause Lyme's disease, are a different story and if untreated can be fatal. The symptoms are common so one cannot be sure unless you find the tick imbedded and are so small that it's difficult to spot them. We haven't yet found any of the tiny deer ticks in the School Forest. However, when Dann and Tim went turkey hunting last week they came home with some imbedded. One has to wait 21 days before tests can be done and then if antibodies have formed, they will need to be on antibiotics for a year.

Late flash. Jay sold his newspaper. Mike and Sue went to provide moral support. On the day of closing, which took hours, Mike babysat with all five kids (his two and their three) while Susan held down the newspaper office because Tuesday is the day the paper has to be put to bed. It never fails to impress me how close and supportive my family becomes when problems occur.

Working part-time and playing part-time equals more than a full-time job, but it's fun.

CHAPTER 17

Sixty-Two and Counting

SEPTEMBER 25, 1989

Dear Cousins,

 Again we have two new additions—Aaron, born on Father's Day to Andy and Kate, and Martha Jean, who arrived the day before yesterday to Tim and Bobbie. Martha missed our birthdays as Dann and I have birthdays five days apart and she came between. Many years ago Dann and I decided to follow the family tradition of naming our children Biblical names. When I was pregnant the first time we selected either Andrew or Martha. The second time we waited for Timothy or Martha. By the third round we were beginning to have trouble because Dann's brothers, who had a head start, had used many of the male Biblical names. That time we chose Jason (Acts 17:5, in case you doubt me) or Martha. For my fourth pregnancy we chose Michael or Martha and then gave up. Everything comes to she who waits although in this case it took 38 years.

 Andy and family drove out from Denver and we got to admire and play with that baby when he was one month of age. Whenever some of this family comes to visit, all others gravitate here so for days I fed a family of 14. Foreseeing this, I had filled my freezer. Each morning after I took the head count I would pull a complete meal from the freezer.

 Bobbie was in labor for so long it worried us, but both mother and daughter are fine. She has two teenagers by a prior marriage and always said she didn't want any more so this surprises and pleases us. It would be a shame if Tim never had kids. I have a mother's one shot philosophy that says you don't stop feeling like a parent just because a child gets married, neither can you hassle them over life's decisions. They all know that I will tell them once when I disagree and expect them to listen. In return they know that I will not lecture a second time nor will I be upset if they follow their judgment instead of mine. I had my one time this summer getting two minutes during which I carefully listed all the moral, religious, and legal reasons why I disagreed with living together unmarried. When I stopped for breath, Tim said, "Okay Mom, I'll take care of it." We're delighted with both our 8th and 9th grandchildren. We seem to have broken the three generation span of males as the female grandchildren now outnumber the males.

After Martha's birth we traveled north to celebrate my 62nd birthday at the cottage. From now on the government starts paying me for living. I looked at that $194 and wondered how many more checks there might be. If I should live as long as Mom did, the government will be sending me checks for 35 years. We celebrated by hiking amidst beautiful fall color in Pattison Falls State Park. All calories that I walked off jumped back aboard when we capped the day with a Triple Treat at Bridgman's Ice Cream Shop in Superior.

Although it was late in the year we traveled to the cottage for several reasons. I looked forward to having some much needed uninterrupted writing time. I have to use a typewriter when there, and switch to the computer when I get home. The last time I turned the computer on it screamed panic messages—disk error, stop, check your disks, do not continue, etc. I had asked for an annual cleaning and obviously something didn't get put back right, but I'm back on line now. Also an insurance problem brought us up north. Our company doesn't like our wood stove. They insisted on changes in the chimney so Dann is up on the roof working while constantly bracing against a brisk wind.

Roof problems also occurred at home, requiring a new roof. As this will be the fourth time, we have to remove the first three. I remembered your stories, Georgiana, so we prepared the best we could, but that's difficult with a full attic. We moved out what we could and covered half the attic with tarps. Workers ripped off that half and then the rains came. Water dripped through and ruined a bedroom ceiling we had just replaced last year. Throughout the night Dann set out buckets to protect our newly refinished wood floors. The work progressed slowly exposing us for two weeks. On sunny days the men began working by 9:00 a.m., took a two-hour lunch break and quit by 4:00. We were frantic, but nothing hurried them. We now have a beautiful new roof, but a ½ inch of litter covers everything in the attic. We'll be cleaning all winter.

When Andy and Kate went home they left Tony, now 11, for two weeks. His short attention span causes difficulty at school and poor reading skills affect everything else. He thought he was getting a two-week vacation with his grandparents. What he got was a concentrated dose of summer school one-on-one with Grandma. I pushed his reading material back to a level at which he could cope. It took five days to get him to even open a book because he hates reading. I used reading/record books and he followed along word for word as the record related the story. I read aloud at suppertime, things like PT109 and Johnny Appleseed and using stories that he read himself I allowed him to barter those for TV time. Following his interest in birds I placed a stool by the kitchen window with bird book and binoculars. I would identify the bird, but he had to use the index, look it up and compare the picture to the live bird using my binoculars.

I talked to three School Forest guides and together we totaled nine grandchildren. We taught this special class our bird special— demonstrated bird adaptations and feeding habits by using our stuffed birds, listened to bird calls on the audible Audubon, handed out binoculars to each child and walked on the Sugar River bike trail. We kept them entranced for three hours. Each child had an accompanying grandmother and every time one asked, "Grandma?" we all auto-matically turned.

We followed this up with taking Tony to the Children's Museum, to the life-size dinosaur exhibit on the Madison campus and to the Field Museum in Chicago zeroing in on his interests—birds and dinosaurs.

We wanted to take him tent camping, but thought it would be more fun with more kids so we picked up Luke and Michelle and took all three. The mess in the attic fascinated Tony and he helped Grandpa empty buckets up there during the "monsoons". He crawled under the screen porch (this requires a small person) and helped drag out Dann's collection of 500 or more hubcaps, which needed sorting. He followed Dann around constantly asking, "What are we going to do next, Grandpa?" He never had time left over to watch TV, which is the way it ought to be. I kept a journal listing what we did, what worked and what didn't and sent it home with him along with three recommendations as they are becoming concerned about his schooling. I wouldn't have missed that challenging two weeks for anything, but we were more than ready to send him back on the plane.

I needed weeds for a Homemaker lesson I am teaching. Dann went with me and we walked along the railroad tracks in a light, misty rain gathering what we could. It was a pleasant walk because it was warm and we were dressed for the rain. We don't often take time to do something like that and it was surprising how many people we met also walking the tracks in the rain.

Instead of another trip this fall we stayed home to go to school. In addition to the Scottish dance class every Sunday night, Dann audits a music theory class at the University, I am attending another Creative Writing class and together we signed up for an intermediate ballroom dance class.

When I get up at 6:15 for exercise class I don't usually bother to take the dog outside, but one morning I did. An inspiring time of day occurs at predawn. The sky was pitch black. Not the same as the black at bedtime as this promised something to come. Stars twinkled around a silver new moon in the southern sky. All was quiet as the world slept. Ten minutes later I finished my coffee, put Ranger back in bed and went outside preparing to depart. What a difference ten minutes made. Only a few stars twinkled, the blackness was less black and a morning haze hovered around the street light. There have to be some benefits of getting up at an awful hour to do awful things.

Here is advance news: we'd like you all to put next July 7 on your calendars. Some time ago, we mentioned that everybody now has wedding dances. We wished we had done that, but perhaps we could consider it for our 50th anniversary. Jason replied, "Heck, Dad, you'd better do it on your 40th, while you can still dance." So Dann proclaimed we are having our 50th anniversary, 10 years early. I read a wedding prayer the other day that ended with "walking together into the sunset." Dann changed that to, "Not us. We're going to dance into the sunset." Great idea if our aching feet will allow it.

We attended a friend's second wedding and this triggered reflections on the ups and downs we have weathered: what I would have liked different or what I would do over exactly the same, the problems of living with someone, compromises, sharing and listening to each other, always having somebody to do things with and the things one gives up for family.

Another friend made the comment one day that she didn't have any family anymore and wanted to be adopted. I asked her how much family she could stand and invited her to our Thanksgiving. She's not bashful and made the rounds visiting with everyone. Luke and Micky stayed overnight which fills up my motel. Micky loved sleeping in my antique rope bed, but as it is quite high she had to be careful not to fall out.

JANUARY 16, 1990

Dear Cousins,

Okay Grandmother Lorraine, we can't compete with you anymore. I have a suspicion that we might be done with our grandchild count. It now stands at nine. It's great to hear from you-all, but why does your letter always land on my doorstep just before Christmas?

Stollen day occurs here one week before Christmas. I made 24 that Dann delivered immediately. I kneaded each batch for 10 minutes by the clock although those 10 minutes got longer and longer. A line-up of warm bread puts us into the Christmas spirit as giving is such fun. I don't know how I managed the years when I baked 60. We gave them for business gifts because we didn't choose to give alcohol and couldn't afford the bakery.

When there were only four days left before Christmas I started sewing Dann's Scottish peasant shirt using an authentic pattern copied from a shirt in a St. Louis museum. This roomy, pullover work shirt from the 1800s was worn by fur traders, fishermen, raftsmen, gentlemen or rowdies and has no pleats or darts only funny gussets that make it baggy. This is like doing income tax—I have to do one step at a time, I can't try to figure out why and can't work on it when I'm tired. Dann wore it right away as we had finally gotten enough nerve to join the Scottish demonstration team. It is one thing to know the dances well, quite another to know them perfectly when performing before an audience. We danced for the New Glarus Winter Festival. The first time must be the hardest. It surprised me to find that I actually enjoyed it.

My family thinks it's time to organize my notes and miscellaneous scraps of paper as the entire family presented me with genealogy software. I spent much time reading the manual, and can see a great advantage if I can figure out how to correlate my notes with the system.

Christmas sped by rapidly. Within two weeks we held five parties, a total of 160 people. I can't resist entertaining when we have such a spacious house. For the first party we invited our TOKEN team from church. This is a group of 23 teams consisting of callers and bakers. Under my direction they make calls where needed—either joys or concerns, do sympathetic or joyful listening and deliver fresh baked goods. I've coordinated this for 11 years. It's unique because we're not asking for money or pledges, simply showing a token of our concern.

The second party was our square dancers. Our reputation has grown making us speechless when the count came in at 64. Moving living room furniture onto the porch, we set up long tables stretching through the living and dining rooms, with additional tables in the study and kitchen. The long expanse of red tablecloths dotted with green napkins gave a festive air to the whole house. My committee helps in the kitchen, everyone else is shuttled upstairs where a fire blazes in the fireplace and hor d'oeuvres tempt the guests. At zero hour we allow them to come down and look for a place to sit. It's the most fun party we do. I love to wander through and admire the house after all is set up. Our biggest problem was: what are we going to do next year?

Party #3 was a progressive dinner for the School Forest Guides with the main course here. We revolved from home to home and ate for three hours.

Party #4 was the Scottish dancer's potluck following their Christmas dance. Dann and I had studied with our checkers all week learning the program dances. Moving checkers helps picture the sequence your feet must go and enabled us to dance 17 of the 18 dances on the program.

Party #5 followed the next day and that's a bit close. Dann and I tried to shift gears from a sit-on-the-floor potluck to a formal Swiss dinner served by my Homemakers. Three of us spent the morning making Kalber Baelleli (veal meatballs). I chose the menu in advance, selected recipes from the chosen country, and passed out assignments. Everyone cooks something unfamiliar to them. This is a hard party to manage because I cannot keep those Homemakers out of my kitchen and I cannot work when they wander through. I worked hard this year so that I could work less—in other words, more committees.

CHAPTER 18

Over the Border

APRIL 8, 1990

Dear Cousins,

My apologies. This missile has waited here while we attended an Elderhostel at the Prude ranch in western Texas. We took classes in Astronomy at the MacDonald Observatory and also attended classes in Mexican archeology and Folklore back at the ranch. We traveled in our Scamper and after the Elderhostel we camped at Big Bend National Park and took two unforgettable side trips. It is impossible to visit the grandeur of Big Bend and not wonder what it's like on the other side of the border. We crossed five times. The first three occurred while rubber rafting through the Santa Elena Canyon. The trip started at dawn, requiring us to travel from the campground to the river before dawn and thus we experienced the magnificence of the sun rising across the desert as it fanned out in all variations of red and magenta. Our river raft stopped three times that day, always on the Mexican side—once to view the Indian pictographs, a lunch stop along a canyon creek, and the third time to climb to the fern grotto. Crossing the fifth time we drove from Del Rio across the bridge, through customs to the adjoining Mexican city of Acuna viewing this city from a locked and moving car.

But crossing #4 enlightened us the most as our curiosity conquered our fear. The idea of slipping across the Rio Grande casually, with no customs, no passports and no car, intrigued us. We tried to bury all our valuables out of sight in the camper,

Dear Cousins

parked on the Texas side, locked it and ambled down the rocky track to the river. Five relaxed Mexicans reclined on the bank. One sat up and pointed across the narrow stretch of the Rio Grande. "You go?" he asked. We nodded.

Another man suddenly came alert. "Amas burritas?" he asked hopefully. Across the narrow Rio Grande we could see the level, rocky beach on the opposite bank. At the far end of the beach six dusty burros tied to a hitching rail were whisking their tails at pesky flies. More dark skinned men sat hopefully and three children raised clouds of dust as they chased up and down the gravelly beach.

"No burros," I replied, "We'll walk." The hopeful look faded.

"Okay, you follow Jesus…shortcut." Jesus was a young boy of about fourteen. He caught my attention because he was clean, much too serious and quiet. He slid down the muddy bank into an old metal rowboat half full of water and started bailing. The man called Pepe clambered down also and untied the boat from the willow bush.

When most of the water had been dumped he announced, "Sit. Middle." I slid down precariously and hopped up to the middle seat where Dann and I huddled together. Water swished in the bottom threatening to cover my shoes. As Pepe pushed us off, I noticed a pencil-sized stream of water pouring in behind Dann's foot. Pepe at one end, and Jesus at the other, picked up oars and began to stroke straight down canoe fashion. The current was moving deceptively fast and in less than two minutes we washed up against the rocks that formed a wing dam on the other bank. Pepe jumped out in waist deep water and tried to pull the boat upriver. We finally just stepped out hopping from rock to rock. Whenever I slipped, two or three hands steadied me—always laughing madly at my imbalance. We paid Pepe the $3.00 agreed upon for the boat ride. As this was supposed to be a round trip, I hoped he would still be there when we were ready to cross back.

Silently Jesus started off on his "shortcut" for the village of Boquillas that perched on a rocky hillside a mile away. He strode rapidly and expected us to follow through the sand and heat, past the mesquite, the loose burros and a Texan longhorn steer, through the dump littered with cans and broken glass until finally he clambered over the big boulders at the edge of the village. Once when I thought we were walking much too fast in that heat, I tried to slow down by asking him to identify mesquite. He stopped for almost sixty seconds while he answered my questions before racing off again. The village consisted of several dusty, tumbledown buildings. Goats meandered up and down the street. A half dozen children of varying size and cleanliness approached us with pieces of a purple crystal saying, "Please senora" and something I could not understand.

We simply responded "No." We walked by the school which looked like it was never open and into the dark church where bird droppings littered the pews and the altar table. We couldn't leave fast enough, but this time we didn't have Jesus to follow. We did okay over the rocks and through the dump, but the sand and mesquite look the same everywhere and in an uncooperative fashion, the burros and steer were now grazing in a different area. After disagreeing about whether we had come on this path or that one, we simply turned our shoes up, memorized our tread and tracked our footprints in reverse back to the river. Our faith in the round trip fare was justified. Pepe still remained. I tottered out on the boulders and jumped into the rowboat. This time Dann took the oar in the rear. He tried to explain to Pepe about ferrying across at a 45° angle so the current wouldn't sweep us downstream, but Pepe responded with only a smile. Finally Dann pointed and we landed at our willow bush right on target. As I crawled into bed in the camper that night I gave thanks I was born on this side of the Rio Grande and not south of the border.

In San Antonio we did more conventional tourism strolling the Riverwalk and re-learned Texas history at the Alamo.

Before leaving home I had hired a new office secretary. Immediately after returning I became aware that unexplained confusion reigned in the office. I couldn't confer with the new secretary because she kept calling in sick. When the bank statement arrived for February, I realized she hadn't even balanced January. We had gone through all of February with an incorrect checkbook balance and had been living dangerously. It took two days of my auditing the entire system to document five instances where cash deposits did not make it to the bank, plus unauthorized checks that were made out to cash and signed by the secretary. I can't tell you how much sleep I lost over this. I was shocked, amazed, felt sick, and finally angry. We changed the locks on the office, put a red flag on our checking account, filed criminal charges and hired a new secretary. This means I am no longer semi-retired, but working long hours trying to redo her work while simultaneously training a new secretary. I have spent all year breaking in new secretaries and am now on my fifth. One couldn't add even though she was working on a PhD, one couldn't handle three jobs simultaneously. Having a secretary only keeps me semi-retired if I can keep her.

We often have Luke and Micky for overnights. I sent them to bed one night and Dann followed to tuck them in. Shortly after, Michelle came downstairs crying, "I told Grandpa I was sorry."

She was followed by her brother saying, "Grandpa sent me for a broom and dustpan."

"What for?" I asked.

"He just needs them." He surely did. They had broken the ceiling light while wrestling on Micky's bed. We deduced they must have been standing on the bed whipping towels in order to reach that overhead light. All was exceptionally quiet after that.

We also had them over April fool's weekend when breakfast turned out to be supper—hamburgers, fried potatoes, carrot salad, apple pie, and orange milk. Luke tackled all with enthusiasm, but Michelle pushed the food around on her plate. I finally asked, "Micky, do you not care for the food, are you not hungry or are you not awake yet?"

She answered mournfully, "I usually eat cereal for breakfast." The orange milk caused her much distress although we reassured her that vegetable coloring wouldn't alter the taste. She was a non-believer. Lunch turned out to be a breakfast menu and I had saved her perfectly good milk so it appeared again. She looked at it with a sick expression and sighed, "Grandma, I just can't" so we fed it to the dog.

When I checked with Mike in the evening to see if everyone was okay, he said the first thing Micky had said was, "Let's have orange milk for supper."

Knowing what happened earlier he had replied, "I certainly don't want that yucky stuff!"

She insisted, "But Daddy, it tastes the same. It only looks different."

I had my last blood draw and wondered why I have subjected myself to this for 10 years. I dislike getting up at 6:15 in the dark, I hate the stress tests. For the detested blood draws I have learned to observe my technician. If she looks experienced I promptly tell her I am a problem child with tiny veins to forewarn her. If she looks like an average technician I grin and bear it in silence, because to tell her my veins spell trouble makes it worse for both of us. However, I always feel better after exercising and am proud that my bone density has increased, instead of decreased, and pleased that the doctor is excited by this research.

Last night was our annual Scottish ball, which attracts people from surrounding states. We housed nine. This fills all the beds even in our big house. It was a sight to see nine of us in our halls dressing simultaneously in ball dresses and kilts. Every mirror in the house filled with flashes of gorgeous plaids. To behold five men in kilts strolling around was also spectacular. A true Scottish kilt has eight yards of material mostly in the back pleats. When the Great Hall at the Union fills with sets of dancers, lines of those gorgeous kilts swing out in unison. We attended a Scottish country dance summer school in Canada last summer dancing for six days, sometimes six-eight hours a day. The rest of the day we spent on our beds in the dorm with feet straight up against the wall or soaking in the tub.

I grieve that this year I have lost my long time friend and former college roommate. Over the years she and I often discussed our respective cancers as both of us underwent mastectomies. This causes much soul-searching as I wonder why some are allowed to walk and some fall. She and I followed the same philosophy after our surgeries. From that fateful day we set priorities and always did first what was truly most important.

CHAPTER 19

Fiftieth Anniversary – Ten Years Early

JULY 10, 1990

Dear Cousins,

Because half of you missed our big day, I'll repeat some of it. We started out with a list of everyone who had filled a special spot during our memorable 40 years. We invited square dance friends, Scottish dancers, Scouter cohorts, Homemakers and many relatives. The list grew and grew. Dann reassured me, "Don't worry. Half of them will be out of town in July." As we worked on party plans we often heard a catchy song on WIBU, broadcasting from Poynette. We hummed along. The chorus aptly describing senior citizens caught our attention.

> "Old Pappy Time is pickin' my pocket, pickin' my pocket.
> I can't make him stop it.
> Old Pappy Time is pickin' my pocket,
> stealin' constantly."

Soon Dann was singing the verses around the house.

> "I used to go a-hunting, I was young and gay,
> Shot a hawk on the wing least a mile away
> My gun is getting rusty and my bird dog died
> Pappy Time has spoiled my shootin'
> and he's dimmin' my eyes."

Before long party acceptances reached 210. Apparently no one left town during July this year. I was floored. Dann was elated. "What a great reminiscence party this is going to be," he declared. "That song fits. Why don't we sing a duet?" I don't have the confidence in my vocal talents that Dann has, but he can be persuasive. He searched all the music stores for the music and found nothing. We drove to the radio station at Poynette and they referred us to Uncle Ozzie who gave us a tape. Again Dann was elated and suggested that I just listen to the tape and write an arrangement. I became more and more hesitant.

I replayed that continually until I could write down the words, the melody, and slowly filled in underlying harmony. The third verse became my favorite.

"I used to take my honey and go for a walk
Got real spellbound, couldn't even talk
I still love my honey, but the flames burn low
"Pappy Time" gives me trouble every day that I know."

I must have played "Pappy Time" a hundred times before the harmony satisfied me. We practiced together another hundred times as I sang the harmony under Dann's soaring baritone. He was elated. I was skeptical.

Dann's cousin agreed to create a replica of our original three-tier cake topped with the original bride and groom figures that had been nestling in an attic cabinet for 40 years. Excited granddaughters oversaw the guest book.

We decorated the hall with royal Stewart plaid. Live musicians played for our wedding dance, but the Scottish demo dance team also performed and taught audience participation dances.

And everybody danced.

Some with Grandpa

Some with Grandma   **And some just danced perpetually**

There were no blizzards, no sudden illnesses, and no airline strikes. Two hundred and ten came from all over the country. I showed off some of our actual wedding presents—the battered, water-stained Betty Crocker cookbook and the guaranteed unbreakable Boontoonware dishes that I dutifully dropped without any advance warning.

Dann spoke about the beautiful friendships we had enjoyed over the years and declared our primary purpose in having this party was to say "thank you for the memories." My eyes flitted from person to person and I realized I was seeing the story of my life. I saw the Scoutmaster, who broke his leg on a Scout ski trip, forcing me to fill in as driver for the trip to the Emergency Room. At the next table I saw the naturalist who had talked me into becoming a 4-H resource counselor at Camp Upham Woods and many of the guides who had done night hikes with me in the School Forest. I acknowledged Scottish dancers whom we had performed alongside on the big stage at the Civic Center. Down the table I found a cluster of Homemakers whom I had taught how to use a microwave. I laughed at the friend who had constantly complained that she had no trees in her yard so we had sneaked in after dark and planted a mulberry tree without owning up to that dastardly deed for 20 years. I sighed over the friend who had vacationed with us up north whom we had to drive to the Emergency Room in Duluth for surgery and her son whose hand explored our cookie jar so often that we called him our fifth son. I sent waves of silent gratitude to the guidance counselor who had persuaded us to take a foster daughter, to the lawyer who kept Dann out of jail when we fought a city building ordinance, to the egg man who helped remove cracked stucco from our old house and towed it away behind his tractor.

I gave special thanks for the table of relatives—for the brother who had kept three sons when we had to hospitalize the fourth while traveling on vacation, for the brother who had taken us into the underwater lab to see manatees, for the brother who had canoe-camped with us on the Buffalo River and the brother who visited every year making a total of eight young male cousins constantly causing a rumpus in our upstairs. I fondly recalled the New York cousins who had hosted 18 of us for a skiing weekend in the Alleghenies, and for Georgiana and Bob who had taken us fishing in Canada every June. That banquet hall was my personal Arabian Nights.

Before the dancing started Dann and I stepped up to the mike once more as we had written an extra verse:

"I used to go a-dancing once or twice a year
My polka or my waltz wouldn't bring a cheer
I met up with the Briggs and their Scottish beat
Now they've got me Scottish dancing on my two left feet."

Thunderous applause filled the room. Audience participation dancing pulled all the hesitant senior citizens to their feet. As people left I heard one declare, "This will be a tough act to follow."

AUGUST 4, 1990

Dear Cousins,

We had company all week following that extravaganza. We traded kids continually so the supper count was always more or less. We took the kids to see the circus train and to Ella's Deli for ice cream, paid the party bills, and worked 10 hours in the garden playing catch-up. Then suddenly we were alone, quickly packed our bags, tied the canoe onto the car top, attached the sailboat behind and took off for the cottage.

This year we drew two back-to-back weeks providing much peace and quiet. We sailed, canoed down the Brule and swam constantly even across the lake. Each day we got more tired and slept later. That is the only place in the world where I can sleep until 9:00 a.m. The last weekend our wee cottage filled to bursting as all our kids came for their cousin's wedding 20 miles away. I had to take excursions outside in the middle of the night because there wasn't an available corner anywhere to put my little "night pot". People slept everywhere. After the wedding we returned to the cottage hot and tired, carried in five sleeping children and then Dann and I walked down to the beach for our last midnight swim. The lake reflected like a mirror. A light mist settled over the water and made the village lights from across the bay appear to be dancing. Eerie silence surrounded us making the night completely ours as we silently swam from dock to dock paralleling the beach.

We came home to mass disorganization because things that were in disorder when we had left abruptly were still in disorder. The table extension leaves, after being used continually for a month, are stored once again. We changed all the beds, wrote thank you notes and have been returning borrowed things all week. The one thing yet to return is my ambition as it still feels good to just sit and do nothing. Dann and I will be talking about this month for a long time. Our memories produced reprints of old events and we added new ones. The large number of friends and relatives who took the time to travel such distances to celebrate with us was awesome. What a gift to have such friendships.

We've used all our spare thinking time for the past year setting this up. Suddenly it's time to figure out "what can we do next?" Goal setting makes our lives challenging and satisfying. We just need a wee bit of rest before we shift gears.

JANUARY 5, 1991

Dear Cousins,

Yes, Hope, we received the copy of Grandpa Hibbard's proposal letter to Grandma dated 1873. Grandpa Elijah was special. I can't imagine anyone proposing like that now which shows that generations change so much it's hard to visualize life back then. That's why we should be writing down things that seem ordinary to us. We'll lose our culture when everyone reverts to cell phones and email. It's good that I write to you cousins frequently. The presence of Tony, aged 12, Alex aged 4, and Aaron 1 ½ has seriously inhibited my writing. They've all left now leaving me exhausted.

Andy has decided to leave Denver and relocate in Wisconsin. His house sale delayed his move a month more than he had intended so they couldn't leave Denver until December 1. On the 2nd and 3rd we received 17 inches of snow. I fixed supper for them every night, but every afternoon he would call with a dismal progress report. They traveled in tandem with Kate driving the car and pulling a trailer. Andy followed with a U-Haul truck. When he slipped into the ditch it took a semi wrecker to pull that big truck out. It took five days to cover the distance instead of the expected two. This made him a day late for a job interview in Delavan so he drove directly to Delavan and we met him there. I walked into the office of my childhood church and said, "Help, we need a mini-warehouse." The woman remembered me, spent five minutes on the phone and secured one. We transferred Kate and all the tired, cold, hungry, complaining kids and mewing cat to our car and I drove home across roads still treacherous, icy and full of potholes. Dann, with his brother and our Tim, unloaded the big U-Haul van as it, too, was now overdue to be returned in Madison, while Andy went for his job interview. Fortunately we got everyone into warm, dry beds here before they got sick, which they did and which I had expected after all that stress.

They stayed with us over the holidays and were here for three of our big Christmas parties. Actually this works. The kids loved the parties and the guests loved the antics of the kids. Our house bounces daily with their enthusiasm. Alex looked sorrowfully at Grandpa whenever he had to go out and asked, "Could you please take a shortcut home because I miss you when you're gone?"

Tony obviously never saw anyone wash her hair in the kitchen sink and asked if he could pour the shampoo. When I said, "Absolutely not," he just stood and watched. Finally he asked if that goopy gray stuff coming out of the bottle was what made my hair gray.

I couldn't resist, "Nope, it's little boys like you that do that."

When move day arrived they loaded our utility trailer, attached it to the Taurus and three cars caravanned out of here early in the morning. Tony and I stayed behind—he was in school and I was glad to stay home. Dann called at 6:00 p.m. to say they were still unloading and had been unable yet to get Andy and Kate's king size mattress up the stair well. Tony and I discussed this as we ate supper.

"I bet your Mom and Dad will sleep in your bed tonight."

"No, they can't—it's too small."

"What do you mean it's too small," I asked. "I thought it was a double bed."

"That's too small. They would have to lie so close together they might be touching."

"But Grandpa and I sleep in a double bed and we like to…" Enough. I stopped abruptly as I saw the trouble I was headed for.

Dann didn't get home until 10:00, tired, cold, a wee bit hungry, but done. He left their house thoroughly disorganized, but that's Andy's problem now. They stayed with us for six weeks and it was fun to again have small children here at Christmas time. However, I am delighted once more not to have to get up at 6:30 if I don't want to, am glad to find the bathroom always empty when I need it, and to find Lincoln Logs only under the furniture instead of strewn across the living room. I love to cook, but enough is enough. Dann told me that I cook differently with extra mouths here. The scales told me that too.

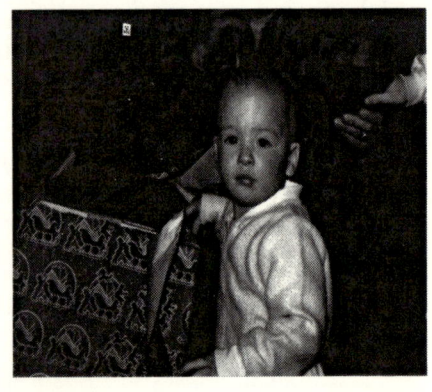

We gave each other matching desks for Christmas. This adds to the confusion as we've tried to shift things. I keep telling Dann to pretend that we are moving and must throw some things out. Tony stood at our shoulders as we went through the desk contents and came up with treasures like baby pictures of his Dad, old bus tokens, Chinese puzzles, and joke books. All the dust gave me headaches for days.

Meditating during Sunday's sermon started me questioning Grandpa Elijah's religion or lack of it. It seems strange to me that a man with his profound thinking (evidenced by his writing), his loyalties and dependability would not sometime have evaluated that decision he made as an eight year-old to become an atheist. I thought that perhaps his Civil War experiences, his love for Grandma Hattie or his sense of family might have changed his mind. I am anxious to start deciphering his journal and wonder if someone, someday will read my journal and wonder how I really felt about life.

CHAPTER 20

How To Retire

APRIL 10, 1991

Dear Cousins,

I labeled last Saturday as black Saturday. First, because I was depressed all day Hope, after reading about your daughter's accident and her problems in rehabilitation. I'm sure you've been a wonderful support to that family during their crises. When one has trouble there is NOTHING like family. Secondly we received a bankruptcy notice in the mail that upset me. We had sold the house, which Dann had built, on a land contract to a young family and they're not meeting their debts. I didn't know whether to feel bad because they are obviously submerged with medical and other bills they can't meet, or whether to feel annoyed because this is the second bankruptcy for them. I suspect they have learned how to use the system to avoid meeting their financial responsibilities. It saddens me to deal with people that feel the world owes them a living and if they can figure out ways to cheat, that's okay. Most of all it depressed me to attend a funeral for a fellow School Forest naturalist. She was four years younger than I and was fine last December, but after four months we lost her to breast cancer. For those four months I maintained a schedule so that every Friday one of our guides spent the morning with her. We did whatever was necessary—cleaning, cooking, visiting or just hand-holding. Funerals from terminal cancer cause me a lot of trouble as I go home saying, "Why her?" Why not me?" The pastor talked about how she had touched the lives of every one of us in some way. I determined to turn my depression around and start touching lives.

We've been thinking about retirement housing. We really don't want to leave these woods and this big house, but can see the advantage of something smaller and more convenient. Dann would like to build a house just for us for a change and he needs to do that now, rather than later. We own a lot that backs up to a park that we've been saving just for this purpose. We want something small and easily maintained, otherwise there's no point in leaving here—perhaps including a home office for the computer, a place for the organ and piano, a fireplace, a workshop for Dann in the basement and possibly a solarium or greenhouse on the south side. The problem is we want to keep everything we have here, but smaller. Looks like the planning is going to take at least a year. I told Dann it would take at least a year to move our 40 years accumulation of stuff but he says, "No way."

We've been doing lots of Scottish dancing. This should have helped the overeating problem I incurred this winter, but it didn't. The demonstration team went out three times in March mostly to ethnic festivals. Sometimes we danced with other performing groups—like the Irish Joggers or the Philippine belly dancers. The trouble with being part of the demo team is that a great difference exists between being able to dance well, or dance perfectly. Even if you know it perfectly, sometimes your mind blanks out in the middle of the dance.

The annual Scottish ball highlights the month of April. Working on memorizing dance patterns, we practiced with checkers over meal hours. Sometimes it seemed as though there just wasn't enough room in my head. If I learned two new dances, three would disappear. I think the intense memorization and constant thinking on your feet keeps you young as much as the seven hours spent dancing on that day—three at the walk-through and four at the ball. I danced only twice with Dann and have learned that when a set finishes, if I just wander across the floor leisurely, somebody will grab me. Scottish dancers are friendly and don't really care who they get as long as they can dance again. In addition to a house full of out-of-state guests, and hours of dancing, an after-ball party follows involving food. Dann and I are always the first to go home, usually by 2:00 a.m. Sunday produces more food and camaraderie when we attend the brunch. The day after is tough. Surprisingly my feet feel fine, as long as I don't expect to stand on them.

We had Tony again for his spring break. We kept Luke, too, for the first overnight and Dann let them sort through his gallon jar of old pennies and take any they needed for their cards. Giving them both binoculars we went out driving and spotted a pair of sandhill cranes, red tailed hawks soaring high overhead, ducks, Canada geese and several hundred white whistling swans migrating through our area. We took Tony to the Geology museum, to see the dinosaur skeletons, to the City Hall to watch the election results being posted, swimming at the YMCA and he went fishing with his Uncle Tim. With his short attention span, it is obviously important for Tony's learning process to teach him on a one- on-one basis. It's fun to have more of our "young-uns" closer—time consuming, but one's life would be empty without children and grandchildren.

AUGUST 1, 1991

Dear Cousins,

This letter should properly be labeled infirmary reports. Dann had prostate surgery three weeks ago and did fine, but last Thursday at 6:00 a.m. I realized he had been vomiting and experiencing diarrhea for hours, dehydrating him to the point that he could hardly walk. Because he had also experienced chest pains I drove him direct to the emergency room. We spent hours there as he underwent tests to check for severe flu, food poisoning or a heart attack. The heart tests came out fine, so they cleared him to go home. The nurse handed him an orange Popsicle and was giving me instructions on his home care when he started to move around which made him sick again. They informed him he had just bought a bed for the night. If it hadn't been for that orange Popsicle we probably wouldn't have made it home before disaster struck again. He occupied that bed for longer than one night

This happened preceding four days of special events which kept me busy canceling. I took Dann out of the demo team dance for the American Players Theater and later cancelled me too as I was afraid to leave him. I couldn't stop the Bed & Breakfast guests we were expecting that night, so asked Susan to go to our house and welcome them. I needed her to invite them to make themselves at home, but she took them home with her instead. I was up early Friday and went out to breakfast with them, to meet my supposed guests and to lend a hand. All were having a ball and the guests were enchanted with the kids. The woman spent her time sketching their old house.

Friday night we had planned a combination Bobbie/Tim blueberry pie birthday party at Mike's and decided to go ahead with that anyway. Dann gave permission as long as his piece of blueberry pie stayed in the freezer. By suppertime my throat was burning. It was the droopiest Willett party I've ever seen. Everybody was wiping runny noses except for Michelle who still had excess energy. She became annoyed with one of the little boys and dumped her coke over his head causing her Dad to send her to her room. If I was a little girl I think that would sound like a fun thing to do, but as I am a grandmother I must admit she deserved her punishment. I decided the best thing I could do was to go home to bed, took my leftover food and departed. Everyone else soon did likewise. I called Dann at the hospital and told him that I might have strep throat as I couldn't swallow, gave up and went to bed.

A battery of tests ruled out things he did not have and the doctor finally said he could go home the next morning. Dann sighed, "That's good, as I am going anyway." He knew that I was ill at home. At 6:30 a.m. the next day when his doctor made hospital rounds Dann, from his hospital bed, set up an appointment with that doctor, for me to go to the clinic. I called my brother that morning, cancelled their planned visit, went to the doctor appointment that Dann had made for me and then curled up in our big recliner for several days. Mike picked up his Dad at the hospital and from then on Dann took over as telephone answerer and chief cook. The first was a big job, the second easy because he wasn't supposed to eat solids and I didn't want to.

We had been invited to a 90th birthday party for a family friend and former neighbor. Sunday was a miserable, rainy day and Dann was still exhausted, but nevertheless, got dressed to go to the party. Mike and the kids dropped in to check on us. I asked if he would like to be a stand-in for a birthday hug so his father wouldn't have to go out and Mike said, "Sure". Dressed in shorts and thongs with a child by each hand, off they went. Many of the guests remembered Mike and all three Willett's were enthralled with the cake and goodies plus the stories the guest of honor told such as the one about May baskets. I had called her one May Day and said, "The boys are en route to your house with May baskets. Please don't eat the popcorn because they spilled it all over the floor, swept it up and refilled the baskets."

Dann and I have practiced togetherness over the last 40 years as we enjoy many of the same things. To be so ill together is a first and I hope it's the last. These health upsets might be longer going away than they were in coming.

We had three mini-vacations planned for spring and summer. Dann carefully coordinated these so that all his pre-admission tests would be done between trip #1 and #2 and the surgery and recuperation between trip #2 and #3.

Trip #1 was our traditional Memorial Day work weekend at the cottage. The guys worked the first day, but on the second day it rained. As that makes a poor workday Dann and Don went fishing. They returned with glistening rivulets streaming down their faces, but grins almost as big as the 29", eight-pound northern pike. One four-year-old immediately claimed, "That's the one that broke my line last night". He learns fast, but I told him that he'll never make a fisherman because when he looked at the steaming fish platter on the table he said, "Yuk". We had planned a potluck for that night so I stuffed the fish and baked it whole dressed with bacon. When I brought it to the table on our biggest platter, that fish hung over both ends.

We stretched our weekend by taking our camper into upper Michigan for a few days after our work was done. We camped at Ft. Wilkins State Park at the tip of Copper Peninsula in pouring rain and fog, staying warm and cozy inside our Chinook while the monsoons raged outside. We spent one night in a National Forest campsite, and one in a private campground—quite different from each other.

Trip #2 was an Elderhostel in the Ozarks on Scottish culture. We stretched the week by starting early, did some sightseeing in northern Arkansas and saw the passion play at Eureka Springs. The performance started at dusk. We sat on the hillside looking down at the city of Jerusalem. It lists a cast of 200 and the show runs for three hours portraying Christ's last week on earth. The marketplace on front stage thronged with people, flocks of sheep, camels, horses and chariots. We viewed the garden of Gethsemane and the tomb on the hills above. Dramatic lighting effects and sound allowed us to keep up with the action. The climatic ending spotlighted Jesus in a fluorescent robe ascending into the sky.

The Elderhostel was superb. We had 18 hours of classroom lectures with Scottish history from 800 B.C. to the Battle of Culloden in 1745. We learned how to roll up in a great kilt or "breachan folah" as they call it in Gaelic. You can bring it up your back and make a hood, or wrap it around your waist to create pockets, or roll it for a sleeping bag. In cooking class we learned how to make Bubble and Squeak, Bridies, and shortbread and discovered in the cafeteria line that southern biscuits come with chocolate gravy. We studied castles, ballads, religion and bagpipes. We viewed the movie Brigadoon, interpreted Macbeth, and learned the Stuart royal lines of descent and the considerable Scottish influence on American history. At the Burns Day Banquet we sang our Old Pappy Time duet with a special verse for Elderhostelers.

Trip #3 was our assigned two weeks at the cottage with no company as we needed to recuperate. We did lots of sleeping, reading and eating and, in between, saw a Chautauqua performance under the Big Top. This performance portrayed the history of Bayfield with pictures and music. We canoed from end to end on Lake Nebagamon and found the eagle's nest. As we were sailing one brisk day one guy wire broke where it fastens to the fiberglass deck. We could only move in one direction, which fortunately was towards home, forcing us to beach the boat for the rest of the week. We sweltered in the blueberry patches, but enjoyed the vivid blue of the blueberries and the bluebells, the purple monarda and wild phlox swinging in the wind, the flame red lily with blazing tangerine centers, the British soldiers (those bright red lichens that so often march in lines on decaying logs), the smoky red of the switch grass as it swished in the wind, the smell of the sweet fern, the "drink your tea" (ovenbird) singing constantly in the distance and the steady drone of the flies. Sweat streaked down our faces constantly, but the swim afterwards and the warm blueberry pie compensated. Swimming daily before breakfast woke us up and dips before bedtime helped us sleep. The cold early morning dip would be followed by a leisurely breakfast of blueberry pancakes with maple syrup or fresh bakery rolls and donuts, or bacon cooked slowly over the woodstove with eggs and Limpa rye toast smeared with homemade currant jelly and orange juice made with fresh pumped spring water and topped with steaming hot coffee. Nobody diets on vacation.

SEPTEMBER 28, 1991

Dear Cousins,

Okay Dorothy, I'm impressed with your track record and am determined to match it by sending this on within 24 hours.

I hate to start with an infirmary report, but we weren't finished when I last wrote. Dann didn't get better and they finally decided he had ruptured himself when he was so ill, so he went back for a third time for hernia surgery. I had never seen one day surgery before. I admitted him at 9:30 a.m. After more than an hour in the operating room we were home again by 12:30. He doesn't remember much about the trip home though.

I had planned to pick up a grandchild in Delavan the next day, but didn't feel I could leave Dann alone. We finally managed to squeeze in the promised grandchild visits the last days before school started. Alex was excited about her visit, her first time alone at Grandma and Grandpa's. She talked non-stop and was my little shadow all day telling Grandpa, "It's fun to do Grandma's chores." She was apprehensive about sleeping alone in the guest room and announced, "You know, I'd really rather sleep with you Grandma." But after I said no she fell asleep immediately.

First all I heard was, "I'm gonna miss Mommy and Daddy," but this morning it was "I'd like to stay here forever." Together we did spring housecleaning in the doll house. We added Michelle as in most cases two works better than one. This theory did not work at bedtime. It alerted me when they came down to kiss me goodnight and informed me, "You don't have to tuck us in. We can do it ourselves." Going up noiselessly a few minutes later I found one twin bed filled with two giggling girls, the other bed empty. I settled this promptly. On the next trip up I found two giggling girls in the bathroom and settled that even faster. Although we had two girl cousins to start with, we followed with two boy cousins. They all helped entertain Grandpa, who was still immobile on the couch and we eliminated strenuous excursions like the Circus World Museum. With beastly hot weather they happily settled for daily swimming plus cooking lessons in the kitchen. I appointed the boys as breakfast chefs. Luke made pancake puffs and Tony put together the rest—Luke worked eagerly and Tony under protest although I think he enjoyed it in the end. They accompanied me to the grocery store and got a lesson on unit pricing. We found a lot of strawberries on the quick sale counter so I decided they should learn how to make biscuits and we had strawberry shortcake for supper. Each boy made a batch and during the meal each ate his and then some of his cousin's shortcake. One boy finally commented, "Your biscuits aren't bad."

The other replied, "Neither are yours." Pretty good when they are usually competitive. Dann tired easily and I repeatedly told him that being hospitalized three times in one summer might necessitate a longer recuperation time.

Although we had plans underway for an extended trip to Australia and New Zealand this fall, this is obviously not the right year so we've planned an easier trip to Florida instead. We'll visit with my brother, explore historic St. Augustine and fly to Antigua for a time share week. We hope this will be restful to have the same bed for a whole week.

Lorraine, I listen with horror to your moving sequence because we may be not far behind you. It's hard to know which comes first—buying or selling. Jason and his wife are going through this once more in St. Paul. Their buying and selling dates don't coincide exactly and Dann expects them to be out on the street shortly. The art of being a good mother to that son is not to worry. He has crises all the time and wiggles through. He is a survivor. It's the process of our moving that worries me the most. How could we have accumulated all this stuff? I keep cleaning out closets while saying to myself—what if you were moving next week? The throw-out pile gets bigger that way. The junk is easy, the good stuff is easy, but what does one do with the stuff that is too good to throw away? Perhaps I could sneak it under the Christmas tree.

Yes, Hope I have been working on *Dear Mom*, but slowly, as it doesn't have top priority. I write People Profiles for our church newsletter plus my daily journal and I have assignments every week for writing class. My teacher claims that the more we write the easier it gets, but I question that. Those words don't come tumbling out easily

CHAPTER 21

Over the Hill and Picking Up Speed

January 6, 1992

Dear Cousins,

I came across a retirement 10-year plan that I sketched when Dann first retired. As we are now five years down the pike it is interesting to review.

1. TRAVEL – We have done well with another trip to the British Isles mainly Scotland and to the West Indies and Nova Scotia. We've covered all 50 states—Oregon and South Carolina being the last two.

2. HOME IMPROVEMENTS – We're about done with this one as we've put on a new roof, fixed the screen porch and redone the little bath and hope we can live with the rest.

3. CLASSES – We have taken classes in dance, computer, Arboretum, organ, sewing, bridge and writing. Also four Elderhostels with classes on photography, folk dance, customs of the Appalachians, geology of the Shenandoah Valley, log cabin architecture, ballads and early instruments, Civil War, archeology of central Mexico, astronomy, Scottish history, clans, cooking, castles, migrations and tartans. We can call this one complete.

4. OUTDOOR RECREATION – There doesn't seem to be time left over after the first three. We keep trying to sail but meet obstacles; but we've canoed some and do travel and camp in the Chinook.

5. HOBBIES – Genealogy goes on eternally, but even a new software program hasn't pushed me enough. My closet is full of

material swatches that ought to be sewing incentive, but aren't. The writing goes full speed ahead. We fished in Canada and on Lake Michigan. Furniture refinishing projects fill up the basement, but they wait unfinished. The dancing goes on constantly.

6. VOLUNTEERING – Mostly church work.

I don't like these infirmary reports. Dann is doing okay and my brother, Frank, as well as can be expected. One week before we were to join him in Florida he called to say he had gone in for a check-up because he was perpetually tired and they diagnosed leukemia. He had one week of chemotherapy before we arrived and then four weeks in the hospital during which he became very ill. Lois, his wife, slept in his room most of the time.

We vacationed in Daytona Beach and St. Augustine, but kept in daily touch. When it appeared that Lois was at the end of her endurance, we asked her to get permission from the doctor for us to enter Frank's isolation room and we drove back to Homosassa. Dann took Lois home, fed her and insisted she go to bed. He did errands, chores, and answered the phone while I stayed in Frank's hospital room. Gradually we alternated with one of us on the home front and one with Frank. When we felt that Lois was rested, we left for our time share on Antigua.

This was our first usage of the Wisconsin Dell's time share week. We won't be using it at the Dell's, but will bank it to use elsewhere. We had a deluxe two bedrooms, two bathrooms, kitchenette and balcony with an ocean view. Antigua has 365 beaches, one which we utilized before breakfast and at bedtime. We rented a car and drove all over the island getting lost every time because there are no road signs. We sailed in our bay in a little sunfish, but also took a day trip on a 45-foot sailboat. I got my first exposure to snorkeling and was grateful for the native who swam alongside holding my wrist. When the island came alive every night with steel bands performing on our beach, we crawled into bed and buried our heads. I have a permanent vision of the West Indies, Antigua in particular as a land of bikinis and steel bands on shimmering white sand beaches, roads laced with potholes, wandering goats and no street markers...of EC (East

Caribbean) money that makes you feel like you're spending a fortune...of strange food like conch roti...a time of no schedules and no hurry...of sudden darkness and no notice rains...of tilting sailboats and the wonders of snorkeling...of swims before breakfast and barefoot walks on the beach in the moonlight...of an open produce market where everybody yells at you to buy their black pineapple, fresh fish or whole nutmegs...of an island full of courteous, genuinely friendly, beautiful black people. It felt good to step out of our world and our lifestyle.

Frank is now in remission and on a program of low dosage maintenance. He has a positive attitude—to simplify their lifestyle and do on each tomorrow what they want to do most, an attitude Dann and I adopted years ago.

I keep trying to write, but unless I give it top priority I'm never going to make it. So reluctantly, I resigned from School Forest guiding. I had 21 years of challenging work I loved, but Dann and I have too many other things that we want to do. Seeing my brother so sick this year vividly brought home to me that I need to quit putting things off.

Pappy Time is indeed pickin' my pocket.

MARCH 11, 1992

Dear Cousins,

We're still thinking seriously about building a new and smaller home as it is considerable work maintaining this huge six bedroom house although one of the fringe benefits of a large house is lots of company. I made a list of all the things I want in the next house and Dann keeps busy telling me why I can't have most of them. The thought of moving terrifies me. We're neither physically nor emotionally up to the task of sorting through 38 years of accumulation. The combination of many closets and a large attic means we threw nothing out and now our chickens are coming home to roost.

When we heard about the snowstorm that dumped 33 inches of snow on northern Wisconsin on Halloween night, we decided to drag out our snowshoes, quickly packed the car and departed for the North Country. Winter in our uninsulated cottage presents obstacles, but lovely rewards including a winter wonderland. Hundreds of dark green pines stood tall tipped with white frosting and snow on the cottage roof drifted two feet high. The yard resembled a desert of shifting sand dunes in pristine white. We shoveled a fifty foot path from the road to the cottage. The cabin temperature showed 22 degrees, colder than outside and even with a fire in the Vermont casting stove two hours passed before we had to even worry about losing heat out an open back door. We shoveled a path to the outhouse, but the wind sweeping through our little valley kept drifting snow back into the path. Shoveling paths has the beneficial effect of allowing one to not notice the cabin temperature is only up to 50 degrees. After it warmed up if we opened cupboard doors blasts of cold air would rush out. The dishes and silver were too cold to hold and tiny ice crystals on the floor crunched under our feet as we slipped precariously across. It isn't as bad as it sounds. We snowshoed, warmed up, and ate, cuddled close to the fire. We cross country skied and discovered how out of shape we are, and at night we walked the road in the deep snow that hadn't been plowed. Orion's Belt twinkled in the starry heavens as we admired the blackness of the night and the utter silence when the wind went down. I found muscles that screamed, "I didn't know I was expected to work like this." We gloated in our warm, cuddly beds in the morning. We sat around the woodstove for hours and consumed breakfasts of slow cooked bacon and eggs, cinnamon rolls, or buttermilk pancakes, strawberry yogurt and maple syrup. We played cribbage and read, and using our eight marked checkers, we practiced Scottish dance patterns. The beauty of winter in the north woods, where nature is not yet changed by the ways of man, filled us with awe.

We found four days to be enough. When we came home I appreciated the thermostat, a faucet that turns on, and a warm toilet seat. When I unpacked my flannel nightgown the smell of wood smoke drifted upwards and reminded me of the crackling fire, the lone chick-a-dee sounding off in the early hours of morning, the wind moaning around the cabin, the smell of bacon on the woodstove, the hot Russian tea warming me all the way to my toes, the feel of aching muscles and the dog's cold nose, the snow crystals sparkling in the sunshine, the black world of the night and most vivid, the silence of unforgiving winter.

We are addicted to Elderhostels, but sometimes we run into problems. For our fourth one we traveled to Tree Haven, the Environmental field center for the University of Wisconsin Stevens Point, housed in their dormitories. Dann woke me at 4:00 a.m. the first night to whisper that he couldn't talk and was having trouble breathing. I knew immediately I shouldn't have made his bed up with the woolen blankets that they had issued to us. I gently removed the blankets from his bunk replacing them with my floor length fluffy bathrobe and his down jacket. Applying hot compresses to his neck in an effort to clear the airways, I talked to him until he started to relax from the antihistamine he had taken. He slept soundly for what was left of the night, but I awoke frequently.

We listened to lectures on the music of lumberjack camps, music traditions of the six Wisconsin Indian tribes, and our German musical heritage. We had a class on instrumentation and learned how to make music on anything—rubber bands, oven racks that we strung with carrots or green beans and drummed next to our ears, forks with wax paper, washtubs, and water-filled goblets. We decided we were not going to get any fresh baking for supper because we were using all the oven racks from the kitchen. When the carrots and beans appeared in our classroom we decided we might not get vegetables either, but when the water glasses and spoons and forks appeared we really worried.

At the evening polka fest we learned dances of ten different nationalities including African and Israeli. We studied Croatian music and learned simple clogging steps and authentic Indian dancing. The Indian teacher talked at length on Indian philosophy. I started with a negative attitude as I didn't want to listen to the problems of spear fishing or reservation drinking, but soon realized I often agreed with him—things such as the Indian respect for the earth and the belief we must change our ways if we're going to preserve the earth, the importance of family units with activities including both elders and youth. He told how he had learned in Sunday school about women being created from Adam's rib and he had accepted that belief, but had always gone home afterward and counted his ribs. I liked his attitude that life is not survival of the fittest, but requires cooperation from all and an acceptance of different beliefs. We danced to the Indian music and drumbeat. We did the life cycle of the fish dancing while squatting on one bended knee with the other leg extended to the side. We did the snake dance, shed our skins and then, although it took four tries, we died and jumped across the line into the hereafter. He concluded by saying that he didn't expect to change our minds in an hour. If he could do that, then someone else could change them back tomorrow, but he did want to leave us with some things to think about. And he did. Between classes we filled our tummies with marvelous things from the bakery, watched the flocks of birds in the feeders, fed the deer and snowshoed.

We are submerged in the selection of a house plan. It has to be special to compensate for leaving this hideaway in the woods. I am asking for: an eight-foot ceiling to accommodate our antique beds, a bay window for my 80 year-old Christmas cactus, a first floor computer room and grandchild dormitory accommodations in the basement. On alternate days we falter in this decision although we both feel we should move while we can do it together. I make big decisions okay, little ones are my downfall. I have ever increasing piles of magazines too good to throw away and will never have time to read them. What does one do with the jammed drawer of recipes that one means to try sometime? And how can I give up the loom that Dad made for me although it has been in pieces in the attic for 33 years? Or Dann's collection of hundreds of hubcaps or all the boxes of Dad's wiring supplies that Dann snatched out of Mom's house when she sold it.

In desperation I tried a new idea. I marked my calendar as vacation designating this to be a week of vacation at home. Dann will concentrate on that solidly packed basement and I on my writing. I don't think this will work, but we can't lose by trying.

We have just finished our annual Scottish Country Dance Ball weekend. This year we offered hospitality to two men from Minneapolis, a couple from Rockford and a man from Chicago.

We spent much time sitting around our dining room table visiting over tea and homemade sweet rolls. This is the real plus of hospitality—getting acquainted with more dancers, the friendliest people we know. By the time they leave two days later, we get engulfed in bear hugs. Often they bear hostess gifts. This year our gift was one-of-a-kind. After dancing for four hours in the morning for the practice walk-through, our Minneapolis guest announced that he would massage my feet. Every screaming muscle in my feet sighed in relief as his thumbs applied deep pressure back and forth and then he individually exercised every joint in every toe. At the after ball party he offered again. Mournfully I said that I had my share already. He countered that he had volunteered to do anyone and all had hesitated and he thought I might set an example. He didn't need to ask twice. My muscles were screaming after the four hours of walk-through, but after another four hours of dancing that night I wasn't sure they would ever feel again. So in the corner of the living room I peeled off my stockings, hiked up my long skirt and plopped my feet into his tub of hot water. A steady stream of guests arrived bearing food and as they passed, they all asked in horror, "What are you doing?"

"We're giving a Scottish demonstration," I told them. He had a line waiting after that. Scottish balls are impressive. A line of men in dazzling kilts that tilt in unison as the dance progresses makes a brilliant and unusual picture. The benefits are many—both physical and mental as we strive to keep up, but the friendships create the best benefit.

I've seen all of you this spring at Bob's funeral. Georgiana, you and Bob with Dann and I have done so many special things together that it's hard to accept those days are over. Dann says some days go by around here when we don't talk about anything but sickness and that gets depressing. I guess this has something to do with our age. So hang in there Georgiana and try to look at the glass half full of wonderful memories instead of the empty part that lies ahead.

CHAPTER 22

Wedding in the Wild

JUNE 24, 1992

Dear Cousins,

Our family keeps stretching. Although Tim and Bobbie have lived together for years and have an almost three year-old daughter, now it's official. Ours is not to question why, but fervently thank the Lord.

This wedding weekend was an "experience." Tim wanted to be married at our cabin with only the immediate families present. This sounds like a good idea until one looks at the logistics. Just our "immediate" family makes a total of 33 and an isolated cabin creates a lot of togetherness. We ate and slept together for 24 hours. Twelve of that 33 were active, enthusiastic young-un's, but even that worked out. Dann and I removed ourselves by sleeping in our Chinook camper. Jay and Mike, with their families, put up tents down on the beach. Andy and family occupied the neighbor's boat house apartment. We gave the bride and groom priority for our guest house and everybody else filled the five double beds, crib, and two couches in the cabin proper.

We arose to pouring rain on the day of the wedding. I heard Bobbie in the kitchen saying, "Darn, darn, darn," but the weather radio promised clearing by noon. And it did. The mosquitoes then came out in zillions. By late afternoon a strong onshore wind, swept them away and the evening sky streaked into shades of crimson. The call of the loons, although coming from a tape, created a north woods atmosphere. Tim and Bobbie stood on one side of the beach campfire, Tim's Uncle Bruce, who married them, stood on the other side as the last rays of sun dropped in the west on the far side of the lake behind them. The bride clutched a bouquet of wildflowers. The family huddled on the terraced embankment and listened to Brother Bruce compare a marriage to the fire as both create beauty and warmth and produce energy. The wedding supper was canned corn beef hash (a family favorite) and a wedding cake that flattened so much it was better described as a wedding cookie.

I promised sourdough pancakes for Sunday morning. As the old oaken table on the porch, when extended, only seats 14 we gave shift preference to those with planes to catch, jobs to get home to, or those with the greatest driving distance. I mixed and Mike flipped and we produced pancakes for hours. After most had left, Mike and Jay's families, along with Dann and I, cleaned and closed the cabin and beach as it would stand empty for four weeks. Many things have occurred at our family cabin on Lake Nebagamon: a baptism, a memorial service, numerous birthday parties, many honeymoons and now—a wedding. The conversation in the women's locker room at the Y on Monday morning concentrated on what a wonderful idea it was to have a wedding around the campfire on the beach. I muttered, "Yeah, but a bit risky with rain and mosquitoes."

"But oh," one responded, "being married is a great risk and how appropriate to promise to love in sickness and in health, in thunderstorms or sunshine and through mosquitoes."

As soon as the wedding was over it was time to make chore lists for the reception that would be held for the newlyweds at Mike's house. Even though Mike and Sue live in the country, 100 guests will tax their facilities. Rain and mosquitoes threaten again and all we talk about this week is inventories of chairs, coffee pots, picnic tables, tent canopies and chemical toilets.

I recall memories of many sons' weddings, all different. For one wedding I went directly from surgery to the church. One took place during a blizzard and many of the guests could not make it to the church. One required planning for over a year in advance, at one the ushers kidnapped the two mothers, taking us to the most awful bar they could find while the bridesmaids did the same to the fathers. Now one around a campfire. I enjoyed each one.

I had almost forgotten that I had submitted my story "A Penny Saved is a Penny earned" to the Yarns of Yesterday contest, but today a letter appeared announcing that it had placed 29th out of 344, and I was asked to attend the recognition luncheon. A thrill, although it would be a greater thrill if I had placed a little higher. I think that story of the depression years would trigger memories for you all, especially Fran and Ede who must have been teenagers at that time.

Last weekend we attended an Energy Fair at Amherst, Wisconsin. We lived in our camper, but we still froze. What's with this Wisconsin winter weather in June? The Fair offered 72 seminars relating to energy and the environment. Thousands of people attended from all over the nation. Most of the instructors are dedicated environmentalists who claim that we can't afford not to use the technology we now have to save energy and reduce pollution. They stressed the necessity of <u>now</u>. With our new house in mind, we attended classes on sunspaces in your home, solar hot water systems, passive solar, environmental lifestyles, super insulation, woodland stewardship, solar food drying and photovoltaric cells. The display of solar photovoltaric cells produced all the energy used at the fair. We have to figure out how to translate this information to the house we want to build. And no, we haven't yet selected a plan.

In addition to thinking ahead towards a new home, I look back and am overwhelmed by years of accumulation. My Homemaker lesson on decluttering didn't help. I am trying to figure out the difference between clutter and personality expression. Some clutter is what makes people interesting or—is it the clutter that makes life interesting?

Last Thursday night, actually Friday at 2:00 a.m., the Fire Department notified us that one of our buildings was burning. One tenant apparently neglected to extinguish his cigarette when he went down the hall to the shared bathroom to take a shower. Discovering the fire when he returned to his room he tried to extinguish it, losing valuable time and then he panicked. The Fire Department arrived to find him standing naked in his doorway, the room ablaze behind him and refusing to move. As he is over 300 pounds it required considerable manpower to drag him to safety. They took him by ambulance to the hospital, and evacuated the other tenants to motels. When we arrived, the Red Cross Disaster van was already there. This van has two desks in the back and a window, like a bank teller's window, where you stand outside and converse with people inside and large drink containers mounted on the sides. The personnel gave out blankets that the tenants wrapped around themselves while doing necessary paperwork. These exhausted volunteers had also been up the night before working on a tornado disaster. This fire had spread rapidly into the wall. Firemen ran upstairs to the apartment overhead, and axed out that wall in order to reach the fire. We had just remodeled that vacant apartment and a new tenant was scheduled to move in the next day. We were thankful Madison Fire Units 1,6,10 and 11 managed to contain the fire even after it spread into the walls. Facing a dreadful aftermath the next morning, we visited our tenant in the hospital, repaired broken windows and door locks so the motel-housed tenants could return, requested an insurance adjustor, but failed to secure a dumpster because the tornado damage of the night before was using every available container. Our tenant will be okay, but he has lost everything he possesses. It will take months to repair that room, but the rest of the building survived.

More than our house here will be difficult to leave. Our yard abounds with wildlife. Yesterday a woodchuck dove under the little shed where he (I hope not she) apparently lives. The raccoon lives in the woodpile. Turning my headlights on him last night he clambered halfway up the woodpile and disappeared between the logs. I know that the chipmunks live in the storage shed because I get scolded every time I walk by. One day I found deer tracks in the garden. The mole constantly crisscrosses over the plowed dirt and the squirrels play tag in the oak trees. Bird song surrounds us when we're watering the lawn—the cardinals and blue jays splash in the bird bath, the robins, grackles and cowbirds walk around in the sprinkler spray, the wha-cheer of the cardinals sound off constantly in the treetops, along with the wheep of the fly catcher, the drumming of the woodpeckers, the beautiful opera-like trills of the wrens, and the ever-changing crying and mimicking of the catbirds. Other springs I have come home after guiding and been so tired from tramping in the woods that I collapsed on the couch. This year is different as I frequently putter outside the rest of the day feeling a need to appreciate this yard and woods while I still can. We cannot duplicate this.

Although I officially retired from School Forest guiding last fall, they just gave me a surprise retirement party. They frosted a cake marking a trail across the top that meandered amongst some trees and gifted me with a beautiful sweat shirt. Using glitter glue and fabric they had appliquéd recognizable oak leaves on the back and equally recognizable poison ivy leaves on the front. Dann wanted to know if they were trying to tell me something.

It's been a long time since we attended a parade, but knowing that Mike and Michelle were riding the Chamber of Commerce carousel, which Mike had fixed, created an incentive. He had discovered on Thursday that the float was broken: the carousel couldn't go around so the music wouldn't play. He asked the Chamber for money for expenses and was told, "There's nothing anybody can do to make that thing work." That waved a red flag for Mike and we proudly watched it roll down the street in perfect operating condition.

Georgiana, we thought about you on Father's Day as the boys enjoyed that special day with their father. For years they missed having a father around for Father's Day because we were always isolated somewhere in Canada fishing with you and Bob.

Challenges fill my days. I suspect I would be bored if it were otherwise. There is something seriously wrong with my computer rental management program as I can't make the cash balance, those end of the year banquets and parties mess up my diet, I can't find time to walk, only top priority things get done, the Homemaker committee meetings are endless although I did enjoy the Scholarship committee. It's fun giving away somebody else's money. We went to Hardee's, where one of the boys worked to tell him he had won. He just stared before asking, "This is a joke, isn't it" This kid is already self—supporting although still in high school so his need is tremendous. We chose him because he wrote that no one in his family had gone on to higher education and he wanted to set an example for his younger brothers and sisters. I have also attended several high school Honors Assemblies to award scholarships. After I got over being terrified by facing a room full of high school kids, I found it gratifying. This counterbalances some of the terrible things kids are doing that one reads in the paper and it restores my faith in the next generation.

A new experience this year was the charter fishing trip on Lake Michigan that Georgiana arranged. I always wonder why I do these things when my stomach immediately starts to slush back and forth, but I climbed up on the upper deck and sat with Captain Jim and then felt okay. It also felt okay to come home with our full quota of four trout (two each).

We timed our garage sale so that Luke and Tony would be here to help. They dragged tons of old magazines down from the attic. We didn't anticipate what a hot item those magazines would be. Priced at 10 cents apiece people carried them out by the wheelbarrow. This is all in preparation for moving, but the attic doesn't look one bit different. Kate, Tony and Grandpa, using odd parts, assembled a working 10-speed bike for Tony to take home.

CHAPTER 23

Traveling the Old Silk Route

SEPTEMBER 4, 1992

Dear Cousins,

The anticipation level here has reached new heights. We're leaving next week traveling as ambassadors for the Friendship Force on a trip to what looks like the end of the world – at least half way around. We're going to Uzbekistan, one of the five new republics that broke off from the Soviet Union. We'll be in central Asia in the mountains and the desert, in Muslim territory and on the old silk route where camels plodded laden with silk as they traveled from China to western markets. Many have asked us why we want to go there and I have wondered about that, too. As Christians we will be a minority. We have a great desire to learn about different ways of life and meet people whose lives differ from ours. We will be home hosted and fervently hope that our hosts speak English. We have been learning a few Russian phrases and have mastered yes, no, coffee, tea, thank you and toilet. This should take care of any major crises. We've also been studying Russian history and the Islamic religion. Traveling in the Third World raises concerns on the part of one son. I reassured him that, at present, there is no unrest in this area and no, I won't drink the water. His parting comment was, "Well, it sounds like a trip that I'd love to take, but I sure as heck don't want my parents going there!"

And no, we're not building yet. Still no house plan. Dann and I have barely been able to converse over this hectic summer.

Twice we've had three sets of company coincide. (Only people living in five bedroom houses can stretch to this.) We loved it, but as chief cook and bottle washer I got tired trying to keep up both at dawn and at midnight.

Here's another tenant story. The average person probably has no idea of the human interest stories that continually pass by a landlord. One of our tenants also worked on Tim's maintenance crew. We knew he had an alcohol problem, but we saw no visible evidence of this as he behaved responsibly and worked hard. One night he apparently sat in his room drinking and chatting with a female tenant. After several hours of this, he raped and beat her and then was shot and killed by the police when they were called to the scene. We pondered whether we should have rented to him or hired him when we knew he had a past drinking problem. After much soul searching we concluded that yes, we should have done exactly what we did. He was trying hard to pull himself back up and he needed the helping hand we offered. He always stopped in the office in early morning for coffee but it just wasn't enough. We shudder at the horrible effects of alcohol.

I have much to do getting ready for this overseas trip. Can't help wondering if it's more work than it's worth. I've had to make plans for our absence in so many places this makes me realize it would be easier if we didn't constantly assume responsibility for so many different things. One good thing about this trip is that it points out vividly how many enjoyable things we involve ourselves with.

NOVEMBER 20, 1992

Dear Cousins,

It took us awhile to recover from our Uzbekistan trip because the time difference of ten hours required catch-up sleep for a week and also because everybody wanted us to present programs. We realized how far away the other side of the world is when we traveled over two nights. The Friendship Force housed us with a University family. Mersaid was vice rector of the University of

Tashkent, head of the Mathematics Department and Computer Science. His wife also taught at the University. Their 22 year-old son spoke some English. The 15-year-old son was learning and we spent a lot of time with these boys. Our Russian words didn't work very well. Uzbeks are proud of having been an independent republic for one year and quickly taught us the Uzbek equivalent for our Russian vocabulary of nine words. We experienced great friendliness and hospitality. These people are anxious to learn about us and for us to learn about them. We've discovered that they are fine people even though they may be non Christians or former Communists. We now read newspapers differently, catching every item about civil unrest in Tajikistan. I came home with three observations: (1) what a shame that we have worldwide language barriers, (2) that I have erroneously attributed such things as brotherly love, consideration and concern for others to Christian living, but many Moslems match the ethics and moral living of my Christian brethren, and (3) it's a small world so we should be concerned about their environmental problems although we don't set a good example. I came home profoundly thankful for clean water that comes out of a faucet and a toilet that flushes.

I read your letter with horror, Lorraine. I know we have to downsize, but don't know how we're going to cope with that. Trips to central Asia don't help because we came home loaded with gifts. People keep asking if I don't miss the School Forest guiding and I can only say, "Sure, because I loved it, but I have too many challenging things to do with Dann."

We both worked at the polls yesterday. A presidential election stretches into a long ordeal. We opened early, but the lines already reached out the door. After one hour, I tore the polling lists in two and split the line into A-L on one side of the hall and M-Z on the opposite side. This enabled us to go twice as fast, but we didn't catch up until noon. After a couple hours working at a slower pace, we again worked up to full speed with waiting lines for the rest of the day. We tabulated until midnight thus putting in a 19-hour day. I don't know why we do this for what we're paid and don't see how the city gets by with paying less than minimum wage. Wasn't it wonderful, though, to get such a high percentage of voter turnout?

And yes, I'm taking the eight-week fall writing class again. It's like eating peanuts, I can't stop. Our first story assignment was to write a story and then go back and change all the active verbs to passive so we could see how that slows a story line. I had a terrible time doing this. When we read aloud in class the teacher commented, "Is that the worst you can do?" It delighted her that some of us had so much trouble trying to write poorly.

Happy Thanksgiving to all of you. After our wanderings in central Asia this fall, I realize how much we have to be thankful for.

It's been a busy year with many trips, a wedding, and many responsibilities in the Manx society and Homemakers. It's hard to find time for writing, but I did. It was hard to find time to study house plans and we didn't. Perhaps next year.

Last fall my writing teacher talked to the publisher of a new monthly local paper called *Dane County Kids* who asked to see some of my material. As a result I am now doing a monthly "Dear Mom" column and learning to deal with deadlines. To see something I have written in print is a soul-searching experience. To realize that strangers are reading about things important to me shakes me up.

I had several new experiences this year. Our church Women's Society always plans one Sunday service. When they needed a female guest speaker for the sermon they approached me. The idea of speaking from the pulpit causes palpations, but the topic they wanted was the Environment and Stewardship of our Earth. The topic intrigued me, but the idea of standing in the pulpit to do this upset me. Dann pushed and the intrigue won out. I chose five problems, four too many, and tried to limit the talk to 15 minutes. I talked about the ozone layer, global warming and CO^2 emissions, importance of trees and rain forests, ground water quality, and disposal management including recycling and did a lot of research. It flattered me later when a young man said he had quoted me all week. From now on I would prefer to leave for Florida when that day rolls around. One joy during that agonizing morning was seeing Dann receive the Women's honorary award for his years of church service—unusual for the Women's Society to cross the gender line.

Things went downhill after that. Dann had been feeling poor, but he got out of bed to come listen to me and then he gave up and shared so we were sick simultaneously. We really appreciate sons and daughter-in-laws who come with soup and movies. When we checked with the doctor yesterday and said we were almost okay he replied, "Okay, two more weeks of pacing yourselves because if you get exposed to anything now you'll blow the rest of the winter." Obviously we need to stay home this winter, to recuperate and think about house plans.

We finally worked out the Uzbek exchange so some of them came to visit us. They were delayed several times as the unreliable Russian Aeroflot overbooked their reservations. We hosted Mersaid, with whom we had stayed and a non-English speaking man named Bahadir, who manages an embroidery factory in Bukhara. Our local chapter programmed their days and took them through the Capitol and Historical Museum, through General Motors and Marshal Erdman pre-fab houses. In addition we took our two guests through the University, the Biotron lab and the weather satellite, visited a bakery and our son's auto body Shop. We hosted the communal spaghetti dinner here feeding 20. We also had a breakfast here so our kids could meet our guests. Luke, our 12-year-old grandson, especially enjoyed our non-English speaking guest. Together the man and the boy pored over the Russian phrase book. Luke would say a sentence in English, Bahadir would say the Russian equivalent and then Luke would repeat in Russian and Bahadir would repeat in English. We took Mersaid to the International center on campus as he was anxious to set up student exchanges between our university and his. This was a great sharing experience.

CHAPTER 24

New Year Traditions

FEBRUARY 10, 1993

Dear Cousins,

    We've started a New Year's Eve tradition—a grandchildren's house party. We invited all to sleep over and seven came. We invited parents only for brunch the next morning so most of them stayed at Mike and Sue's and had their own New Year's Eve. Tony, our 14-year-old, arrived first and he and I worked out a tentative brunch menu. The rest arrived by supper time in the middle of which I requested a family conference and announced the brunch plans. Six pairs of eyes riveted on me as I explained, except for four-year-old Martha who, awed by her cousins, was content just to nestle on my lap. Excitement bubbled over and everybody had ideas for what they wanted to make. Food preparations filled my kitchen all evening. Whenever the disorganization swelled to more than I could stand, Dann produced another movie for the VCR and sent everyone in to watch while I cleaned the kitchen and reorganized. Putting the two little girls to bed at 10:00 took a lot of time so before going upstairs, I set up triple activity centers and charged Dann, as expediter, to keep things moving. This was a great example of multi-tasking. It required grinding meat for the traditional Willett hash, activating the air popper to make popcorn for the movies, and having Tony set up on the computer screen to print the brunch menu. Dann's assignment was to keep the five working kids constantly working and they did—all evening.

At midnight we lined up the children still awake and prepared to ring in the New Year with our old farm bell. This bell was mounted on a 12-foot pole next to the driveway. The chill factor that night was -40, but the kids threw on coats and rushed outside. Seniority to ring the bell came by age so Tony stepped up first, gave it one jerk and that old bell boomed across the yard. Luke grabbed it next and a louder clang split the air. Shivering from the cold, Allison stepped up next, standing slightly offside. As she started to pull on the rope, the old bell came crashing down at her feet. We stared at the deep groove in the blacktop that the sharp edges had made. We stared likewise at her stance offside and gave thanks that she was not directly below. Apparently the chill factor had caused the bell to break into smithereens. Any idea of starting a new tradition of ringing in the New Year at midnight with the farm bell stopped. Although the bell died that cold night, the bell post remained and now a rural mailbox rests way up on top. As it is 12 feet in the air, Dann felt it appropriate to paint AIR MAIL across the side of it.

The brunch was an outstanding success. When the parents arrived they were greeted by aproned chefs who seated them, took orders and served them. Each numbered chair had an order blank to fill out.

Chair # _____ WILLETT'S RESTAURANT
HOW MAY WE SERVE YOU?
Multiple Choices Okay

_____ WILLETT HASH WITH EMPTY NEST
_____ WILLETT HASH WITH EGG IN THE NEST
_____ Tony's Texas Toast and Maple Syrup

_____ Luke's Lovely Liver
_____ Michelle's Magnificent Blueberry Muffins
_____ Allison's Amazing Almond Rolls
_____ Elara's Excellent 3-minute Eggs
_____ Grandma's Great Grapefruit
_____ Martha's Marvelous Milk
_____ Trevor's Tasty Tea
_____ Grandpa's Russian National Drink
_____ Orange Juice
_____ Orange on Half Shell
_____ Cocoa
_____ Coffee

ANYONE NOT CLEANING HIS OR HER PLATE HELPS WASH DISHES!

Hugs and kisses okay for tips.

Some of the adults ordered everything. The question of the day was—is this going to be a new tradition? I love having grandchildren close by. It's also good that I can send them home when I am ready. I had misgivings beforehand about trying such an ambitious venture, but it worked.

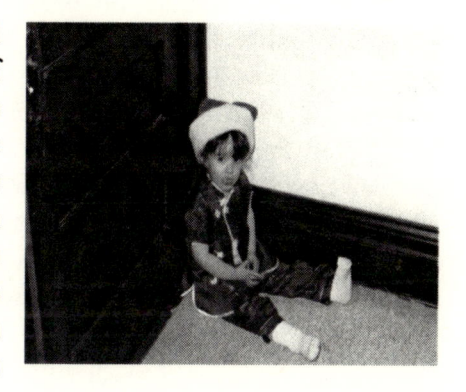

APRIL 22, 1993

Dear Cousins,

Good timing to pick this up out of my mailbox as we left the driveway for Georgiana's wedding. It entertained us for most of the drive to Lake Geneva. This is a good opportunity to give those of you that were absent, an account of her second wedding.

She looked beautiful in a white suit with red blouse and white cap. Among other things that Georgiana and I share is our belief that all things important should be done with red. Brother George gave her away. Many little ones, great-grandchildren, tore around constantly. A steak dinner at Johnny's Supper Club followed the wedding.

I sat next to a 93-year-old lady who captivated me with her stories of homesteading in Wisconsin. She talked about being raised next to the Indian reservation and learning how to ride bareback with the Indian kids. She could remember the year the Kickapoo flooded and they had to evacuate. I told her she should write these extraordinary things down for her kids, but she sighed wistfully and said that she doesn't have any family. Dann and I decided that we need to visit you soon Georgiana and call on that lady in an effort to preserve some of her stories for posterity. I only got the tip of the iceberg that night.

Following dinner, George performed as master of ceremonies and called on people to give speeches that he had requested in advance. When he called us he had said, "Anything goes – a toast or a roast, serious or funny or just get even if you want." And Fran, what we did that night takes away forever the title you once gave me of your "little timid cousin". Dann and I decided that too many speeches can be tedious so we sang our duet. Remember the duet that we sang at our anniversary celebration several years ago? The chorus went something like "Old Pappy Time is pickin' my pocket, pickin' my pocket, I can't make him stop it." Although appropriate for our 40th anniversary we felt it equally appropriate for a wedding of two senior citizens. We sang the original verses and encouraged all to join in on the chorus, which they did enthusiastically. However, Dann had written a new verse that we added,

"We used to go a-fishing in a very small boat.

Weather didn't stop us, just added 'nother coat,

Georgiana caught the big ones and the rest got away.

But the biggest fish she ever caught is the one she caught today!"

The entire room exploded and we had to wait before we could even finish the last chorus. Sorry about that, Georgiana. It was too good an opportunity to miss. After all, I did preface my telling with what a neat, sisterly cousin you have been.

Unfortunately the wedding weekend was also the Saturday of the Madison Scottish Country Dance Ball. We hosted two dancers from St. Paul; one was staying in the Twin Cities for six weeks on business from Berlin, Germany. We sat around the teapot Friday night listening to what it was like when the Berlin wall went down.

Over breakfast on Saturday morning we discussed the economic problems of East Germany. We showed them where we hide the house key and requested that they take care of the dog and then they left for the dance walk-through practice and we left for Georgiana's wedding. The formal ball started at 7:30 that night. We got back to Madison by 10:00 p.m. so we missed 2/3 of the dance, but enjoyed the last six dances and I did dance with our German guest. Without too much difficulty, I dressed appropriately for both a wedding and a ball as we had no time to change. Dann had it tougher. He had a choice of either showing up at the wedding in his kilt or dancing at the ball in trousers. So for this year, the kilt lost. We danced until midnight and then adjourned to a home for the after-ball party tumbling into bed at 2:00 a.m. After our traditional Sunday morning Scottish brunch our guests departed and Dann and I collapsed. It was a truly glorious, but jam packed weekend. Georgiana, I wouldn't miss your wedding for anything, but next time, please try to avoid the Scottish Ball weekend.

This month I fulfilled a long standing promise to take Mickey's third grade class to the School Forest. We started down some mucky trails with eagerness. Gentle, warm winds promised spring soon, while hundreds of snow white Dutchman's breeches stretched as far as we could see across the forest floor. A few bloodroots aggressively thrust through the dry oak leaf litter, opening their faces to the sun and a few sky blue hepaticas spattered the brown forest floor. Because these kids haven't had an environmental field trip before, I covered everything. I told the old Halloween story pointing out how to distinguish white oak leaves (round like ghosts) from the black oak family (pointed leaves like witches hats), but I concentrated on teaching concepts as I love that best. A dead woodchuck demonstrated the importance of recycling and interrelationships. Hibernation teaches the preservation of energy. Studying the old open grown oak we visualized the Indian fires and prairies 150 years ago and imagined the future as for lack of sun that oak forest will slowly change to climax forests of maple. We took apart owl pellets we found underfoot, identifying mouse bones and discussed predator-prey relationships. Mickey was a delight. Being with her peers, instead of tagging behind older cousins or a brother, she acted like the mature third grader she is.

The next day I did another freebie, returning a favor. I took out 12 home school parents to Owen Park and showed them things they could do with their kids. Again, I taught concepts and stressed that they didn't need to know the answers. They only needed to get the children excited enough to raise questions. The kids can research the answers themselves.

In answer to your queries about my "Dear Mom" column, these columns require a lot of work. Whatever story I'm telling has to be limited to 800 words. It's tough to be neither less nor more. I edit each one at least five times before I'm satisfied. Living with a deadline always stresses me. Some of this embarrasses my kids, but they're getting used to it and pick up the paper the minute it's out. My writing teacher says at this point she isn't finding many errors in my class assignments. It's about time as I've looked at those red scratch marks she makes all over and wondered if I was learning anything.

We have given lots of programs on Uzbekistan. We set up Dann's slides with my narrative alongside and I notice nobody ever goes to sleep even in the darkened room. It continually surprises me how universally interested everyone is in the former USSR provinces and their problems. We met a young couple when the Uzbek exchange was here. These people are Uzbeks, who live a mile from us. He originally came to America as an exchange student, but now works as an engineer for the state. She has lived here only four years coming after an arranged marriage that took place in India. She speaks limited English. I took her to my Homemaker meetings and there we encourage her to speak, and gently help with unfamiliar words. After she passed her naturalization exam and became a U.S. citizen she related many of the questions she had studied. It makes me ashamed that I would have trouble with some like "who was the 16th president" or "what are the freedoms of the Bill of Rights?" I will never again take my American citizenship casually. Last month she told us about her arranged marriage. She said she had prayed fervently for the entire nine months that lapsed between the arrangement and the wedding. She met him four days prior to the ceremony. They are Moslem.

We have tried repeatedly to telephone our friends in Uzbekistan. An 11-hour time difference means that we have to place the call from 2:00-3:00 a.m. We got through four times and received a recorded message in Uzbek. Although we hung up quickly it cost us $20.

This should be labeled history year as we have two historical events in August. We've held Willett reunions at the Nebagamon cottage every 10 years beginning when the cottage had been in existence for 50 years. This year we celebrate 70 years and I have resurrected 70 years of fascinating history. I questioned several of Dann's brothers to put together a written picture of those 70 years. They remembered making homemade root beer. After bottling and capping they would lay the bottles on their sides in the wheelbarrow so for three days they could roll them out in the sun each morning and roll them back into the boathouse at night where they covered them with blankets to keep the chill off. When their procedure was a bit off the bottles would explode. They told stories about the clothes washing process when the boys carried buckets of water that would be heated over a wood fire on the beach. The old Maytag wringer washing machine, stored under the house, would be rolled out onto a small cement slab .and then, of course, buckets of hot water on the beach had to be carried up to the Maytag. This didn't happen often as there wasn't much washing to do. How could this be with six young boys? They informed me that they only wore overalls, no shoes, no socks, no shirts, and no underwear. The overalls didn't often get dirty because usually the boys didn't bother to remove them before jumping in the lake. Every night three to four boys would be assigned the chore of walking three miles to Farmer Jones for milk at a nickel a quart. Some boys carried two bottles, some carried one. If you were one of the lucky ones that carried only one that left a free hand for throwing cow pies. Their Mom baked bread making eight loaves each time using a collapsible oven on top of the kerosene stove burners The family made that three-day trip to the cottage only at the beginning and the end of the summer with six boys plus two adults filling all available space in the car. The two little ones were relegated to sitting on the steamer trunk riding backwards, the dog and rabbits were secured on the running board in a luggage carrier and the bird cage was suspended inside the car swinging violently the whole trip.

Immediately following that weekend we will celebrate the 100th centennial of our church. This also involves a lot of Willett history as Dann's grandfather was an original trustee. Dann and I volunteered for the steering committee and we try continually to get people excited about this. We encourage turn of the century dress so when I gave a program last week on the centennial plans I dressed appropriately. We proposed printing a history book, a reenactment of special events, and a mass choir. I wonder what it was like to attend old Trousdale Methodist 100 years ago before they even had a building—or to go to prayer meetings where people ranted and raved against or for prohibition. Or to live in a time when you weren't allowed to do anything on Sunday; neither go to the store, cook, nor read. Walks and lengthy church services were all that the trustees allowed on Sunday. People clearly picked up the spirit of this centennial as we thought back 100 years making us realize how we have changed. One hundred years from now I wonder what will be different.

I find all history fascinating. I got a new diamond ring several months ago—that's the ending to the day when I came out of the pool at the YMCA with an empty setting. Hindsight is useless, but it is sad that we never realized the need for special insurance. That ring endured 40 years of bread making, throwing clay, dishwashing, chlorine pools, and garden dirt. My hands are always getting involved in some mess, but that diamond always twinkled reminding me how important Dann and I are to each other. Now I have a new one with a different history—a very old diamond set in a new modern setting. This was my Mom's and perhaps her Mother's before her. I wonder, as it sparkles at me, about its past and its future. What kind of life did it observe as it was worn by perhaps two of my ancestors? Did it get dirty too? Was it a happy woman that wore it or did it often see tears? Did she live a life of hardship trying to survive in frugal times? Perhaps this one won't get as dirty as at 65 I do a lot less things with my hands. But it reminds me constantly there are many ways to say I love you.

CHAPTER 25

Home Schooling

JULY 15, 1993

Dear Cousins,

We've now attended a second annual weekend at the Alternate Energy Seminar at Amherst. With predictions of violent storms all weekend and a headache threatening, I showed my age when I couldn't sound enthusiastic. Two sons' families were going to attend. Although Dann and I would live in the Chinook camper, all the rest would be tenting. Calling one son I asked if he wanted to call it off. I should have known better as those kids were brought up in the tradition of "camp whatever the weather". It's the violent winds and the flood warnings that worried me, but all went well and we picked up more ideas for our energy-saving house.

You "older" cousins are all wrong. I, too, need to build up steam as I have been in the hospital twice in the last two weeks. When I went to see the doctor after developing pains in the calf of one leg, he suspected a blood clot and sent me in for a test as an outpatient.

They found nothing and sent me home. During the night I woke up with horrible chest and side pains. We had a storm that night that took down half of a black cherry tree and blocked our driveway. Dann attacked that with his chain saw clearing the driveway and then took me to the Emergency Room. The staff obviously thought that a blood clot had moved to my lungs, took tests all day which turned up no clots, so they decided I had pleurisy of lungs and admitted me overnight. Antibiotics cleared up the chest pains, but when my leg continued swollen and painful, my doctor, still convinced that I had a blood clot, sent me back to the clinic for more tests. This time they found a clot near my ankle and kept me flat in bed for six days. I can't ever remember being hospitalized when I didn't feel sick. I felt like flotsam caught by branches in a river at flood stage. I could observe life swirling around me, but with my swollen right leg propped up on pillows I was about as mobile as a cement block. I entertained much company, invited small visiting granddaughters to cuddle up next to me and they went home happily declaring they had "driven" grandmother's bed. I entertained my roommate's grandchildren with Moffett (the teddy bear that Michelle had insisted on loaning). The kids wound it up endlessly so that it would do its thing and play "Rock a Bye Baby".

Being bored I quickly learned all the staff's names and teased them mercilessly, especially the blood draw people who came every six hours around the clock. I delighted in warning them that they would have a tough time finding my small veins. They would blast into the room at 6:00 a.m. for important things like temperatures and after thoroughly waking us, would comment we could go back to sleep because breakfast wouldn't arrive for two hours. Getting up, for me, meant cranking up my bed, turning on the bed light and doing some writing as those two hours were the only time all day that I would be uninterrupted.

I selected a few special friends for daily wake up calls explaining that as long as I had to be up at 6:00 a.m. I thought they ought to rise and shine at least by 8:00. I learned how to stretch my limited horizons without ever moving that elevated foot. I could hook my good foot over the edge of the bed and lean out the other side to barely reach the curtains thus allowing my roommate and me either communication or privacy. By rebounding things off the bulletin board I hit the wastebasket 99% of the time. Wiggling all over the bed helped with those awful back pains as my system objected to so much inactivity. The computer blue box that dripped heparin into my arm fascinated me, especially the messages as it announced "air block", "infusion complete" or "on battery". I did not complain the night of the tornado warning when they evacuated us into the central hall because that meant I got to sit in a chair for one hour. They lined us up in the hall where I could see my next room neighbors. Supper trays traveled with us and one man commented that this was like a community supper. I watched lots of CNN coverage on the Midwest flood conditions. I missed spending time alone with Dann, missed my own bed and going to the bathroom instantly when I needed to. I did not miss my friends and relatives. They were all there, instantly and repeatedly. Do NOT send me a get well card. I am obviously home and not sick. I can drive again and swim and hope the doctor will let me dance soon. I will be on anti- coagulants for several months so perhaps Dann is now living with a time bomb. But hasn't he always? We had had other plans for this summer.

We missed our first week at the cottage because of this, but managed to get our second week taking along two grandsons. On the theory that we needed to get rid of their excess energy we encouraged them to swim constantly, to help tow back runaway rafts, to pick blueberries in the sand barrens accompanied by the multitude of bugs. We all picked strawberries in the Oolu strawberry patch under noonday sun and the boys jogged on the back road. By the end of the second day they were still going strong, but Dann and I were pooped! Their highlight was swimming and they managed three to five times a day. They actually requested a wake-up call for the pre-breakfast dip (and that can be darned cold) and begged for skinny dipping before bedtime (even colder).

They polished up their diving by practicing at least a thousand times off the raft, learned how to deliberately tip a canoe and right it again, how to get back in using one of them for human anchor and how to gunwale (standing on the sides and pumping to produce forward motion). They watched Grandpa fillet their fish, learned that after lunch is naptime for grandparents and that if Grandma keeps putting out scrumptious meals; it takes boys a long time to clean and straighten the kitchen afterward. They learned how to play cribbage and that you can't beat Grandpa at Hearts. They can beat him at Spite & Malice though and delight in being spiteful and showing malice. They learned to recognize the call of the immature eagles perched on the point, and the distress sounds of the ducklings on the lake when the adult eagle spreads his wings and swoops. They learned the call of the barred owl when Grandpa would call him in at night and then he (the owl, not Grandpa) would perch just above the cottage and keep trying to get Gramps to say it again. They could recognize the smell of blueberry pie in the oven and learned that fresh strawberry shortcake with whipped cream melts in your mouth. We delighted in having Luke and Tony with us. Now we need another vacation in order to rest.

We continued to keep Tony for seven more weeks so I could help him with his reading problems. He went home on weekends. I estimated we did about 36 hours of one-on-one tutorial reading. I learned too as I tried to understand the whys and wherefores of the special exercises he was doing. He never resisted this. I guess the joys of having Grandma's complete attention for two hours at a whack counterbalanced the struggle to learn. I was picky, stopping him whenever he didn't say it exactly right, letting him break the word into syllables and try over. I hope he keeps doing this when Grandma no longer sits next to him. I tried to impress him that he needs to ask for help right away when he doesn't understand and not just keep on doing it wrong. I only wish I could have done this for him years sooner.

We have been getting our share of monsoon troubles. Dann and Tim sandbagged our apartment building that borders Pheasant Branch Creek just before it enters Lake Mendota. We anticipated trouble as Dann estimated we could take only another two inches of rainfall. Many of the city beaches closed because the contamination level rose too high. They closed the Tenney Park locks, huge hunks of floating bog have broken off and we counted 40 of those floating islands cruising around in the bay. We have been asked to flush toilets less because the sewage system is overloaded. Yesterday I noticed that our white front door pillars are mildewed gray.

I've been interviewing church members and because this is our centennial year, I picked a lady whose memories of our church probably go back farther than anyone else. When interviewing, Dann and I learned to listen instead of telling our own stories, which we love to do. I have learned what questions get us past that "there's nothing interesting about me" stage. Dann has the ability to talk to anybody about anything when conversation lags. Once this lady got started her stories drew imaginary, vivid pictures for me: how she watched the Capitol burn in 1904 from their front window, how she walked miles to Sunday school on wooden slatted sidewalks. She jumped up and down on those slats to make the water underneath slurp and splash up. . .how she went to church with her father and sat in the Amen corner, how the children had to give memorized recitations at the Sunday School Christmas party. She remembered walking the trestles across Monona Bay to get to Central High and could visualize the stills in the Triangle area. She expressed sadness at not finishing high school because her father didn't believe in education for girls. So many things she talked about are already foreign to our thinking. After writing this for the church paper many people approached me saying, "I never knew all that about Alice."

Our steering committee works continually to keep the centennial "spirit of '93" dangling in front of the congregation. We surprised them this week by roping off the church to what must have been original size and made everybody sit in that small area. For the committee meeting I produced cookies from my 100 year old cookbook.

August 30, 1993

Dear Cousins,

The four-day Willett weekend at the lake went off as planned with swims across the lake, aquatic volleyball, a communal potluck and family talent night Using three boxes of mix, I had made and decorated a birthday cake copying a picture of the cottage. We had an open house breakfast in our Chinook and hoped that all of our eight Willett's would not appear at the same time.

The 100-year celebration at church also went off as planned and included: an old fashioned ice cream social in period dress with a wandering barbershop quartet, a tea where old friends visited and dunked their old-fashioned cookies, a re-enactment service duplicating the first service 100 years ago, a lunch with turn of the century prices (35 cents), a pictorial history of Madison displayed on the walls and period hymn singing.

All that extra tutoring truly filled Tony's summer. I worried, needlessly, that he would get bored. Actually he thinks Grandpa's house is exciting all the time—and it is. We upgraded our Y membership and enrolled him in swimming class and certified him to do weight lifting. I started him on paint by number again and inveigled an invitation from our bicycle repair man for Tony to help build wheels and test drive bikes that the bicycle man had repaired. I got him involved in other kinds of things like: vacuuming, washing the car, care of the dog and cooking thus making it possible for me to spend time with him. It left little time for me to regenerate, but I am reminded how much I do enjoy teaching kids. Now with all the grandchildren back in school and all the celebrations over, perhaps we can redirect our energies to starting that dream house—a scary project because, like this summer, every good thing has difficult aspects to work through, which is what makes life challenging.

CHAPTER 26

The "Green" House

OCTOBER 13, 1993

Dear Cousins,

    Summer, full of events, rolled past rapidly. September more so as we finally selected a house plan and we're underway. Dann re-designed our favorite plan and a retired friend drew the blue prints. We spent weeks discussing what we had to have and what we had to do without. If we leave our present special house, we had better move to another special house. We determined that everything essential needs to be on first floor. Although we'll have a loft with two bedrooms, we kept the master bedroom and my computer room on first. Floor to ceiling glass to utilize passive solar covers the south side of the living room, the skylights help with that and a semi greenhouse, again with south facing windows attaches to the dining area. We're going to race with winter, but if we can dig that hole by November 15 before the ground freezes we will continue to work all winter.

    My calendar officially declares September 12, as grandparent's day, but I label this as grandchild week. We tried to watch Tony compete at cross-country and drove to Burlington in pouring rain, after they assured us that they never cancel only to find that they had. Later that week, he did run and is beating his own record, snapping at the heels of the senior Varsity. It is great to see him trying hard as he has been indifferent for so long.

    When Luke came to visit he commented, "Grandma, I need to collect 50 insects for school. I thought you might like to help!"

"You bet," I replied. So I am thankful for warm, sunny weather yesterday productive for bug hunters, grateful that the big bumble bee flew up in anger when I clapped a jar over him instead of dropping down and out of the bottle and that I have a grandson who doesn't hesitate to ask Grandmother for favors like this. All the nets, hand lenses, charts and books that I brought kept us busy. I miss doing this outdoor stuff and as I dragged out my boxes of equipment stashed in the back of the closet I wondered what to do with my accumulation of teaching aids. I have stated firmly that Dann cannot move his junk to the new house, but mine isn't junk. I just don't need it anymore except on isolated grandchild days. Families are fun when they're not running cross country in the rain—birthday gatherings and bug-hunting get a higher rating with me.

I find it easier to struggle with decision-making in the morning although it interferes with breakfast. Black or white is easy; gray decisions wear me out. Every morning we face lots of decisions, some more than others if we made wrong ones the day before, but we learn fastest when we fail.

Yes, last year I reached that golden 65th that we look at as the age of retirement. Ten years ago I watched friends retire from 40 hour/week jobs and I worried how they would find thought-provoking things to fill their time. All my life I have worried about the wrong things. Now that we are supposedly retired, I can't figure out why we don't get anything accomplished with all that extra time.

A short nap after lunch shouldn't wreak havoc with the entire day. We work slowly and often not in the evenings, but what happens to the rest of the day? Perhaps we're simply catching up on 40 years of never having enough time. I have sorted through piles of stuff on my desk. Next I'm tackling the fruit room downstairs stacked with things that have been waiting for attention. The attic will be the crowning touch for throwaway projects. This week is "Get ready to move" week. In desperation Dann is clearing the basement while I am trying to empty the sewing room closet. The enormity of all this makes us cranky. Each morning we plan to give priority to our MOVE project and afternoons we keep free for the rest of living. Sadly this doesn't work, but I guess we have to try and fail because we are succeeding a wee bit. Not trying would leave us with two choices—everything would either be sorted later or thrown without inspection. We advance by inches. We have miles to go. This reminds me of dieting when one must show dramatic results quickly to provide impetus to keep struggling.

As I attempt to slow down I stop often to listen to the sounds in my yard.

6:00 a.m. Early enough that only the birds and I are awake. The wha-cher of the cardinal, the squawk of the blue jay and the frequent chick-a-dee calls from the spruce tree start the singing. Crows sound off from the top of the tall white pine and a chipmunk emits a steady chirp, chirp.

8:00 a.m. Even though trees surround us I can still hear the cars roaring down the hill, bumper to bumper as sleepy drivers wend their way to work.

10:00 a.m. Next door the school doors slam open announcing recess. The yelling of happy kids fills the air, terminated by the shrill bell calling all back inside.

4:00 p.m. Helicopter rotors reverberate loudly overhead as Med Flight makes it way to University Hospital.

6:00 p.m. Voices and music drift from the neighbor's patio as they relax after work.

9:00 p.m. The yard quiets again. Only the crickets continue to chirp steadily and occasionally a barred owl calls from deep in the woods.

12:00 p.m. Just beyond our fence tires squeal as teenagers show off their new found driving ability making donuts on the school parking lot.

I vow to slow down and listen more often.

JANUARY 11, 1994

Dear Cousins,

Our new house progresses slowly. Wisconsin winter weather held off and we dug our hole, poured basement walls and backfilled the ground before hard frost. We're using information from the Alternate Energy Seminars we have attended the last two summers. Words like thermal walls, passive solar and green space bounce through our conversation. Outside walls will be a sandwich construction of chipboard on the outside with a five-inch core of Styrofoam glued and pressed between the chipboard. This will give the walls an R factor of 27 with an R-41 in the ceiling, and use 80% less lumber. It bothered me when we traveled in British Columbia to see those gigantic logging trucks loaded with two-hundred-year-old Douglas fir trees. We can't keep doing this to the environment.

Special vents in our little three-sided attached greenhouse contained chemicals that pick up heat to 80 degrees. When the sun goes down, the vents release that heat back into the room. The special Styrofoam walls will be cut and built at the yard. At the proper time, they will arrive with cranes and be put up in three days. I asked Dann if we should put things on hold for two months, but he said he didn't mind working in the cold, as that is better than rain. However, extreme weather does slow us down.

I made a list of things that will not go with us—including family heirlooms and antiques. Giving each son a list I requested them to check things they could use and double check anything they really wanted. What are apparently strong family ties surprised me when much of the list came back marked by all four sons. The problem is not how to dispose of extras, but how to do it equitably. The little things are the hardest. I found Dann's mother's old wooden recipe box in the attic. When we closed her house 30 years ago Dann's brothers were about to throw it out, but I snatched it thinking I could take out the family favorites. As I haven't even opened it in all these years I took it to Mike and suggested he and Sue might like to look through it, take out a few recipes and throw it. Susan immediately asked for the whole thing saying she'd make it into a book. I told her that would take years, but that didn't faze her and that file gets another generational reprieve. We chuckled reading the recipes that called for ½ cup of bacon grease and the winter ice cream that you make on the back porch.

I worked on reducing other things, too—namely me. I like to entertain and can't bear to throw out leftovers so I keep getting rounder and rounder. My attitude of "I will do it next week" doesn't work and in desperation I signed up for Weight Watchers. Perhaps if I work hard I won't have to give them money for long. I stand in front of the mirror saying, "If I can stick to this, my reward will be in just looking."

Last fall, I planned an International Style Show for our Homemaker Holiday Tea. Soliciting Homemakers from all over the county who had international dress I signed up 21 entries. Three were men: a Norwegian bridegroom, a Moslem from Uzbekistan, and Dann in his kilt. The men stole the show, of course. Dann taped background music typical of each country for each model. This proved to be such a monumental job that night after night I kept asking, "Are we having fun yet?" I didn't answer yes until the show was over, with no major glitches. The many foreign costumes created in us a worldly togetherness.

We squeezed in a trip to Seattle although we rushed through too fast. Now I have a list of places like Vancouver Island and the islands in Puget Sound where we need to return and do it right next time. We stayed at two Evergreen Bed and Breakfasts, but the highlight was making contact with Scottish dancers on Friday Harbor. We traveled over by ferry. Because the last ferry back to the mainland left at 8:00 p.m. and their dance class continued until 10:00, the teacher took us home for the night.

Back home, dancing at a surprise 40th birthday party for one of our Scottish dancers, Dann twisted his knee and almost collapsed. As we were the lead couple in the set, a dancer on the sidelines immediately stepped into Dann's spot and another stepped up to support him off the floor. For 24 hours he could barely move. Sadly the next day was the ethnic fest at the Civic Center and our demo team had practiced hard for this. As another dancer became ill with the flu at the last minute, substitutions for two people had to be made minutes before the performance. In frustration one experienced dancer finally complained to the instructor, "You have changed my gender three times in the last five minutes. Please stop."

We danced on the big stage this year and when I heard the loudspeaker announce "curtain call for Scottish dancers" my stress level erupted like Mt. Helens, but we managed – even with the last minute changes.

The next day was our digging date. Although we had thought they probably wouldn't keep it, they did. As Dann couldn't drive I was drafted to chauffeur for the week. It turned out that he had injured his hamstring tendon. Between my blood clot and his hamstring we've had a tough time keeping on our "toes". He's okay now, but dances only the slower dances and is being extra careful because we can't afford to have our general contractor out on sick leave. By the end of that week we had a hole, sewer and water, and footings and I am learning rapidly all about thermal walls, face brick and mechanized skylights.

Deer season descended on us, stopping construction for two weeks. Andy brought down a big doe. He claimed it wasn't his because the doe he shot was going in the other direction, but nobody else was near. It's a good thing that when Dann sees blood on the ground he tracks it, because he eventually found the carcass.

We celebrated Thanksgiving at our house again—with all four sons and all nine grandchildren. The youngest generation slept on the floor. We added little Martha overnight as one more didn't make any difference. At dinner time I didn't have enough nerve to put the kids in the kitchen where they would be out of sight so instead I seated them at a long table in the living room in view of the adult table. I insisted that two fathers sit along the side of the table where they could see the living room and this worked.

When I watered my houseplants after the holidays, I decided that plants, like me, droop by the end of December. The hours of darkness stretch too long and after so much excitement, some of us are perpetually tired. During January, the houseplants and I revive as we head for spring.

CHAPTER 27

The Big Hole

MARCH 30, 1994

Dear Cousins,

    We were pleased to be able to attend another "senior" wedding. You are going to have an impressive blended family, Lorraine. Your second wedding reinforced my theories that as circumstances in our life change we must change also to fit those circumstances. This is what is going to keep us from getting old—whether it's a change of residence and lifestyle or a different partner. We need something to look forward to right down to the last station.
    I did double duty people-sitting yesterday. I sat with brother Don after his triple by-pass accompanied by granddaughters. I thought he was probably too sick to tolerate those two, but they were staying with me that day because their father and grandfather were running hither and yon doing necessary errands. I prepared to haul them out the door the minute their voices raised to their normal high pitch, but they didn't, so I didn't. Their great uncle enjoyed listening to their quiet chatter as he drifted in and out of consciousness.
    "This picture is his present. That's a fishing boat, but the boat on the bottom is a sunken treasure ship with gold spilled all over."
    "Uncle Don, why don't you blow that inhalator up to the top instead of stopping at only 2,000?"

"Grandma, I liked watching the nurse beat on him, but now nothing is going on and I'm bored."

"Why does Grandpa always wear orange on St. Patrick's day?"

As I tried to explain Catholicism and Protestantism I got unexpected help from under the bed covers. "That goes back to the days of protestant King William of Orange." And with an agonizing groan, "How did I ever agree to this?"

I had a ready answer. "You sound like a woman who has just delivered her first baby!" It was a long day.

Yes, we slowed down working on the house during the winter. I determine how fast construction is moving by how often I wipe mud from the kitchen floor. We quit every time the chill factor drops below zero, which it did repeatedly. However, our "house" has arrived. The walls, made in Fond du Lac, are polyester cores compressed between chipboard, giving us exterior walls with no studs. The truck arrived early Monday morning. By Tuesday afternoon standing walls reached second floor level. Dann, Tim and the crew have been laying out the interior walls and its shape changes drastically every day consuming all our waking thoughts, especially those long wide awake periods in the middle of the night. It requires daily inspection on my part because things change so fast. One day I walked into my new bedroom and could see the view out the bay window and also what a tiny box that computer room looks like. I can check the closet space and figure out what goes where, or worry about the square footage in the dining area, or the location of the pass-through. That pass-through in the kitchen is designed to allow me to listen in on what's happening in the living room. One day I told Dann, "I've changed my mind. It's too small. I don't want to move."

My brother-in-law laughed, "Reconcile yourself to living in a house. You've been living in a barn."

I made a list of things we'll be doing for the last time. All the kids will be home for Easter weekend. The following weekend we will host a brunch of 40-50 Scottish dancers and that should be the end of massive entertaining in this massive house. I regularly go to bed with a book and bundle of firewood, knowing I will never again have a fireplace in my bedroom.

Did I tell you that Dann has designed the first floor ceilings at 8'1" to accommodate our antique bed that stands at eight feet? Years ago I worried we could never move out of this old farmhouse with its nine-foot ceilings that accommodated our heritage bed. He rashly promised, "When the time comes I'll build you a house for that 100 year old bed." And he has. I'm getting a personalized house as he raised the first floor ceilings to eight feet one inch. I managed to crawl up to the second floor yesterday. Big holes gape here and there, no rails, no stairs—only a wobbly ladder. Once was enough for me.

A miscalculation with the walls made it necessary to drive to the factory at Fond du Lac once more. We arranged for brother Frank and Lois to drive down from Appleton and meet us halfway for dinner as we haven't had time to visit with them lately. This gave us a couple days rest from the construction as we are almost ready for our second D-day when the crane will arrive and hoist the trusses into place. Half the neighborhood periodically checks our construction. I can't decide whether that's because of our unusual construction or because we've proclaimed for two years that we were going to do this, but procrastinated.

The idea of building a house with many innovations doesn't bother me. The idea of moving leaves me panic stricken. I have moved only twice in my life—small moves. I don't think I am going to like it.

With Dann at choir practice I entertained his brother and wife showing them the family tree placemats that I created years ago. I tried to answer his question "What relation was so and so to me?' and then couldn't resist bringing out my box of Grandpa Elijah's 100 year old journals. Reading through terse comments for each day, one feels how different life was when just the wind direction for the day took on importance. Questions arise in my mind such as: did he use a pen with a detachable point and bottle ink? Or I'm entranced with his thoughts upon his 32nd birthday as he asked at what point a boy matures into a man and he reflected that for some, this didn't happen until the other side of the river. This surprising comment came from an avowed atheist. I wonder, "Will my grandchildren be reading my journals 100 years from now?"

On Valentine's Day I expounded in my journal and gave it to Dann. How do I love thee? Let me count the ways: when you touch me holding my hand during grace, warm my cold feet in bed, bump my foot when we're swimming laps or brush shoulders as we clean the kitchen, put your hands around my waist to see if I've lost any more weight or hold me in your arms while we dance...when you ask me how was my day and listen...when you enjoy me reading stories at the supper table or when you encourage me to do things that I'm afraid to try and help when the going gets tough...when you provide me with delightful grandchildren.

Love comes in all sizes. Fifteen-year-old Tony, special because he was the first, because he is so affectionate and always welcomes a hug, because he needs us all to slow him down, to build up his self confidence and help him want to learn. Thirteen-year-old Luke special because we get to see him often, one who achieves easily and will try anything until he gets it, who has a great sense of humor, as when he uses his allowance to buy Grandma a rutabaga because he knows she hates them. Eleven-year-old Allison so special because if she had been born a few years earlier she probably wouldn't have survived, petite but living a normal life because of the surgical repair to the hole in her aorta wall done before she weighed ten lbs. She also holds the distinction of being the first girl in three generations, nine-year-old mischievous Michelle wanting time alone with Grandma especially in the kitchen; just turned seven Trevor, our tempestuous football fan and three weeks younger, Alessandra all ruffles and non-stop talker, my dollhouse cleaner-upper. Five-year-old, Elara, who couldn't wait for kindergarten, demanding one's entire attention often, hard to beat in a card game. Four-year-old Aaron, our busy, curly haired towhead, much too busy with the mysteries of computers to pay attention to grownups and Martha, two months younger than Aaron, special because, I think, she's the last. She can talk her way out of almost anything. Valentine's Day was a great time to realize how special all our nine young-uns are, how blessed we are to see all of our family so often.

When Mike and family arrived for supper last night a disappointed grandson asked, "Grandma, how come you have store bought cookies in the cookie jar?" Why indeed? Because then I'm not tempted so much. Warm, homemade ones are beyond my capacity to resist. One of the sacrifices required by Weight Watchers.

June 14, 1994

Dear Cousins,

It makes a full weekend to have April Fool's Day, Daylight Savings time, and Easter all on the same weekend. It meant we had grandchildren here for April 1st for green milk and dirt cake. Luke and Alli insisted on baking cookies, but when they produced a recipe with yeast I vetoed that and instead gave them an old family favorite recipe. They filled one cookie with bits of paper intended for Grandfather, but somehow Grandma mixed it up when the cookies came off the pan so the kids never knew who got Grandpa's doctored cookie because the recipient never told.

Jason was washing parsnips when Alli and Michelle asked if he could please move the car as they wanted to play on the driveway. They asked three times and each time he responded, "I have to finish what I'm doing first." When he finally went outside he discovered in astonishment that his car had been moved. As the girls walked despondently upstairs on their way to solitary confinement, I overheard Michelle tell her older cousin, "I told you so."

We inveigled as many people as possible up to the attic for "search and give-a-way" hour. I piled boxes in the kitchen and on Easter Sunday invited people to remove their belongings that had assumed permanent residence in the attic for years. Allison ended up with Andy's rock collection, Bobbie took most of the puppets, Andy claimed many of the pinewood derby cars, and Tim's clipper ship ended up in the trash. We still have a thousand miles to go.

Scottish Ball weekend is always busy, but three houseguests and the Sunday morning brunch filled the weekend. Again I looked at people in every corner of my house and thought "this, too, is the last time here." One guest placed everyone in a circle on the floor and sang a song he had written the night before entitled "A Moving Song". It was about the Willett mansion and how they all loved to come and sit and eat bagels and cream cheese, but now the Willett's were building somewhere else…but that's all right because if you bring the bagels. I'll bring the cream cheese and we'll still all go and sit. This almost made me cry.

After all those parties I paid the piper at Weight watchers. This is a long process anyway, but today I went in the wrong direction. I'm beginning to hate Thursdays and don't eat much on those days.

That day was also Tony's 16th birthday. I remember so clearly 16 years ago when Andy called us in the middle of the night and said "soon" and then when the baby's heartbeat stopped the doctors did a caesarean delivering him in minutes. I am grateful that Andy's family now lives closer.

No, we haven't finished our house, nor sold the old one. We reached a milestone when the exterior doors arrived as now we can lock up. Standing open caused us anxiety after last weekend when kids entered during the night with raw eggs. In the process they found the caulk guns full of glue and liberally sprayed some of the screens and the new fireplace. No matter how fast the guys work, it seems slow. Occasionally we have seven men working, but mostly it's down to two as during the summer Tim and our maintenance crew have much to do on our apartments.

The week of the trusses came and went. This is a waiting game. Everything was set up for early Monday morning, but at 7:15, Dann discovered the trusses were not finished. He cancelled the crane, but it was too late to stop anybody else. A full contingent of workmen arrived, putting in only a half-day. Dann rescheduled for Tuesday, but woke me at 4:30 a.m. saying, "Everything is covered with snow and ice. I can't let workmen go up in these conditions and will have to cancel again." We finally made it on Wednesday when the trusses were quickly hoisted up and this rapidly changed it into a house.

We listed the old house for sale a week ago and got an immediate call from a University professor in Michigan. He planned to fly over the next day until we discovered he expected July 1 possession. That cooled him off and lost me half a night's sleep until Dann said, "No way!"

People keep asking our moving date and I answer, "Mine or Dann's?" He figures September because people often move before school starts. I think there is no way we can wade through the basement and attic before October. How does one collect so much stuff and how does one decide? You are right, Dorothy, about not needing so many things, but we will take endless memories with us.

Building a house brings constant problems. The Baraboo carpenters were careless so the greenhouse wall is crooked. The architect had the wrong figures on the blueprints and the skylights arrived in the wrong size. We discovered our Baraboo crew doesn't have Workman's Comp. Under our policy if anything should happen we would be responsible. Weather continues to disrupt as we cannot have shingles delivered in pouring rain. Still the structure changes every day and my imagination knows no limit. The wildflowers that I planted somewhere between the pines a year ago have showed up—intense blue cilia's, my prize twinflower bursting with white flowers, a showy trillium next to it and I recognize the foliage of trout lilies and mertensia.

Michelle came for the weekend and I assured her that she has a dirty Grandmother. We crawled around in the garden planting peas, beans, sunflowers, daisies, coriander, basil, dill and parsley and we spent the afternoon in the attic playing a new game called, "I wonder what's in here?" Michelle went home with a new doll, one box of stuff went directly to the trash and one pile is ready to move to a new address. A dusty job like this done on a hot day was naturally followed by purple cows (grape pop with ice cream!)

Exciting things keep happening at the site—the arrival of the fireplace and conferences over the stained glass owl window, which will be outstanding. We officially added Tony to the payroll for 10 days as Dann discovered menial jobs for which he is reluctant to pay carpenter wages. Tony proudly caulks in the basement and enjoyed watering down gravel for the garage floor. He bubbled with enthusiasm when he got his first payroll check yesterday. With difficulty I persuaded him that he shouldn't walk around with cash, that perhaps $5 was enough to carry.

CHAPTER 28

Are We Coming or Going?

SEPTEMBER 8, 1994

Dear Cousins,

    Sorry this robin has rested here too long. Extra thinking and decision-making for the new house blows my organization. I've been studying wallpaper books and meeting with landscapers, creative window designers and kitchen planners. This business of always having the old house in a showable condition with little notice constantly raises our stress level. Dann plans on moving this fall whether that house is sold or not. As our new basement is done we've been moving things into that basement every weekend. The first thing we moved was Dann's huge hubcap collection. All those hubcaps went directly onto the shelves he had designed so that they could be stored on end and easily identifiable.

    Two weeks in July at our cottage temporarily obliterated all building progress. It's unusual to get two weeks back to back so we grabbed them. We needed to relax. Time becomes unimportant at the lake. Weather becomes more important. Things don't happen on schedule and the weather messes up any schedule that we do set. We frequently slipped directly from bed to our before breakfast swim. One early morning patches of mist hovered on the lake's surface and with nary another creature stirring the lake belonged to us at that hour. The frigid water rippled slightly as we cut our way down to the second dock. Miniscule clouds skittered around us and the far shore blurred. The temperature of the water gradually warmed if we kept moving or perhaps it was just that our bodies cooled down to that temperature. At any rate it soon became more comfortable and the stimulation thoroughly woke us up.

This was our 44th anniversary and although it always seems like we should celebrate our anniversaries with just the two of us, it never works that way. Andy and his family came for the first few days and Jay, with his family for the last five. On the last night Mike, with 16 Scouts and Scouters turned up unexpectedly in the rain. They were halfway home from their canoeing trip in the Quetico and as it was 4th of July weekend, no campsites were available. Soon eight little tents squatted in a row on the old beach road. The place immediately turned into pandemonium. One Scout came to the cottage door looking for scrap lumber because one of them had jumped on the pier breaking two boards They read the Turn out the Lights sign in the outhouse (Dann's private joke) but couldn't find any electrical switches. A forlorn little Scout appeared at the kitchen door to say that he had been putting a new roll of paper on the roller in the outhouse when he dropped the roller down the hole. His "friends" had cheerily volunteered to hold his ankles so he could search for it. One Scouter accidentally locked Mike's van with the only keys inside. It was nice though that when the tree crashed pulling down electric wires one of the Scouters was an electrician. I endeared myself by showing up on the beach with warm brownies.

This vacation encompassed many culinary treats. We couldn't restrain ourselves in the Oolu strawberry fields and were astonished when we came out of the field with 60 pounds. We froze those destined for the home freezer, and the rest went into mammoth, daily shortcakes. Blueberries picked laboriously on the sand barrens melted into pies and often fresh fish turned up for breakfast. We celebrated our July 9th anniversary on a cruise among the Apostle Islands stopping briefly on Stockton Island.

Years of vacationing here on Lake Nebagamon are loaded with memories. Starting with our honeymoon we've been here for a memorial service and a wedding, a 50th, 60th, and 70th birthday for the cottage celebration, corporation meetings and work weekends. We have enjoyed it as a family of six, then just two of us and then two plus grandchildren. We have used this as a stopover en route to our Canadian fishing, to the North Shore drive, to Duluth's Skyline Drive, Radisson's rotating restaurant, Superior's Ore Boat Museum and Bridgman's ice cream. We took day trips to Pattison State Park, Amicon State Falls and the Bong museum, to the Chequemagon tent shows, and to the Red Cliff Indian reservation where we slipped our canoes into Lake Superior and paddled across to make camp on Basswood Island. We regularly swam three times a day and fished in between. We sailed in old Chuck, in our sailing canoes, in the Grumman and our own Day sailor; canoed all the fingers of the lake and down the Brule and inner tubed part of the Brule going over Big Joe Rapids. We've spotted fox, skunk, bear, bobcat, raccoon, muskrat, woodchuck, eagle, beaver, deer and an army of chipmunks. We've sweated and swatted bugs while picking blueberries back in the swamp, hopping from hummock to hummock. We've pumped trillions of buckets of water and cut endless pieces of firewood. We've shivered in the dead of winter traveling on snowshoes while enjoying the serenity of this place. We have absorbed the beauty of the fall while bow and arrow hunting. Most of all we've enjoyed the many minutes of doing nothing as we've relaxed in the rocking chairs in front of the wood stove, in the hammock or around a campfire on the beach enjoying magnificent sunsets. During the numerous storms we sang around the out-of-tune piano, worked every jigsaw puzzle in the cupboard and taught even the youngest to play our traditional family card game—Spite and Malice making sure they learned the spirit of the game that gives it its name.

Dear Cousins

For two weeks I filled in at the office because our secretary was on vacation. My garden produced so abundantly that after mornings in the office, I filled afternoons trying to keep ahead of the produce. It's great, and will be welcomed this winter, but right now it's another load of stuff to move.

The most unusual part of the summer was a visit from Heather, a 21 year-old girl from Bristol, England. She is Dann's second cousin twice removed. Her mother wanted to give her a special birthday present and sent her to us for two weeks. This was the wrong year for that and she was not an easy guest. She wouldn't eat most of the food I offered, never volunteered to help and wasn't interested in much except TV, rollercoaster rides and our 22-year-old step-grandson whom she decided to marry after he took her out twice. I lost sleep over that as I thought grandmothers shouldn't be caught in the middle of those things. This challenged my capabilities as a gracious host to the limit as we took her to the Cave of the Mounds, rode the ducks at the Dells, to Ella's Deli for ice cream, Scottish country dancing, swimming in Lake Mendota, to the Mall of America in the Twin Cities, a Celtic Fest and a movie shoot, and then, we all wore out. Never again will we accept company for two weeks.

Company for the last half of August changed to the four-legged kind as we offered to keep Anna, Jay's 80-pound Rotweiler for three weeks. I hoped that counter smells around the perimeter might discourage the wildlife population from harvesting my garden. I underestimated Anna. Walking out to the garden one morning, in spite of gently falling rain and mud underfoot, I wanted to pick rhubarb from along the edge. Looking up in dismay I saw that Anna had followed me, jumped the rabbit fence and was walking around in the middle of the garden.

171

"Anna," I hollered, "come out of there right now!" Unfortunately she tried. From the center of my immense garden all 80 pounds of her took to the air remaining aloft for only half the necessary distance, which landed her in the middle of 36 tomato plants. She immediately tried to take off again coming up inside one of the metal tomato frames that easily passed over her head and wedged tightly across her broad shoulders. She panicked, throwing her body frantically in all directions knocking down and trampling frames. Tomatoes flew like fireworks. Finally getting out of the tomato patch she desperately rolled on the zucchini vines to knock off that darned thing. As my state of shock lessened, and in spite of not wearing garden footgear, I jumped the rabbit fence to join the fray. By the time I got to her she was trying to dig under the lima beans, but quieted instantly when I laid a hand on her head. Even with her cooperation I struggled in the rain and the mud to un-wedge that wire restricting her front legs. The next morning, after the rain had ceased, I picked up a half bushel of tomatoes in varying stages of ripeness and lined the shelves in the basement with sparkling jars of green tomato mincemeat and tomato relish. Anna has more than fulfilled my expectation of leaving scent around the garden to discourage resident herbivores.

Things kept getting worse so I pasted a note on the back door that said, "Say no," and we did—no trips, no parties, no church, no Scottish dance and no writing class.

Occasionally surprises occurred. When we finally cleared the attic the drudgery became memory lane. We viewed with dismay the dusty wonder of our packed third floor attic that stretched from one end of the house to the other and from the slanted roof in the front to the dormers in back. We sorted into four piles: what was going with us, what was going to the kids, what to give away and what was clearly trash. We thought we knew everything in that attic—wrong, wrong, wrong. At our age our memory may be lessening, but things must have slipped in when we weren't looking. We thought we could identify everything. Wrong again. Some things defied all description, but most brought back countless memories and a lifetime flashed by as we pawed through those fragile, belongings. Our attic was our history book.

It's been a summer filled with company—not compatible with house building. We desperately need a couple more months of good old Wisconsin Indian summer. I doubly appreciated each day this last summer: the screen porch especially at breakfast time, the dark nights, the best garden I've ever had, a yard full of brilliant red and white begonias and impatiens, my huge kitchen constantly in operation emitting smells, a house that stays reasonably cool even when the outside heats up unbearably, five working bedrooms and waking up in the morning to a vista of oak trees waving outside my window. I know it's getting close to time to go, and some days I am sad.

We finally set a moving date and then hoped we could make it. Otherwise all our help would make other weekend plans and we need all the help we can round up. So October 22, it is with the following Saturday as a slide date if necessary.

We have so many September birthdays that we tend to lump them together, but this year Martha's was special as I gave her my old doll house. We left some of the fixing up for her Dad to do, but Michelle and I sewed extra curtains, Dann glued the broken furniture and I re-stuffed the chair made from an orange crate. The most moving innovation was the ornate gold framed certificate that now hangs on the doll house living room wall. If one lies on one's stomach on the floor and shines a flashlight into the back of the dollhouse living room you can read: "Created in December 1933 for six year-old Jean Hibbard by her parents and brothers. Given on: September 22, 1994; to: six-year-old Martha Jean Willett; by her grandmother, Jean H. Willett."

New construction is like moving an elephant. It is a mammoth project, we need people working on all sides constantly, but often that elephant just sits down and we push or pull with no results. Today was one of those elephant-sitting days. Absolutely nothing worked. I started a countdown on the wall calendar. It says only 27 more days which panics me.

CHAPTER 29

The Eagle Has Landed

January 13, 1995

Dear Cousins,

Twice we set moving dates and cancelled because the new house was not ready. Finally on the third choice, we did it anyway. In Wisconsin one faces two inevitable events that we needed desperately to avoid: deer season and winter. We cleared deer season by seven days. We must have had behind-the-scenes intervention with the weather because Madison set a new record for no early snow.

Twelve of us with seven vehicles plus two trailers coped with the task. One car would pull up to the front door, 12 people would empty a room, load the car and then that car would move down the drive. This procedure would be repeated six more times before the fleet could depart. It required three trips. Moving from a large house to a smaller one presents problems and soon stacked boxes filled all the rooms in the new house. This blastoff would have been impossible without supportive friends and family of a younger generation. We agree with one granddaughter, "Grandma, let's never do this again." We've tried to keep this teeter-totter balanced with sadness at what we're leaving behind, but counterbalanced with anticipation at moving into a house that we designed and constructed. We're thankful for continued good health in which to enjoy it, providing we ever manage to get those boxes unpacked.

It took six days to get our occupancy permit because the balcony railing was not completed. We moved in without it, but could not sleep there, temporarily using a friend's spare bedroom. We finally secured the permit hours before the Willett crew left for deer season, so I slept there at first by myself. I decided if I could manage the lock on the front door, I could handle it.

Some things we had to have before moving and we somehow got them. Some things we thought we had to have, and discovered we could live without. I had a kitchen with running water, but no hot water so no dishwasher, no refrigerator or freezer, a stove but no microwave. I had a bathroom with operating toilet and tub, but no shower curtain and no window shades which meant we took baths only after dark. For a while, no washer and dryer, no TV and no hall carpet. But we are here and enjoying our new house immensely even with disruptions.

The workmen were underfoot for four weeks after we moved so I had to struggle with people at my door early in the morning. Men laid my kitchen floor when I wanted to cook. We still have one bath non-operable, one phone not hooked up, a couple dead outlets that shouldn't be, no shutters for the front of the house, a few missing cupboards, unpacked boxes in the closets and no birdfeeders or outside thermometers. I have learned that my new washer empties water into the stationary tub alongside. But if I leave anything in the stationary tub it plugs the drain and sprays the entire room like Old Faithful. It took two drenchings before we learned that. We learned that the thermostat is programmed, but doesn't understand sunshine. On sunny days the bank of 16 windows on our south side shoots the temperature up quickly. I need to listen to the morning weather forecast and turn the thermostat down before the sunshine turns it up. We slept in the guest room last week so we could gauge the heat on the second floor with all the registers closed.

I will enclose a few pictures of my little green space adjacent to the dining area that both I and my plants love. The great horned owl stained glass window was done by a fellow naturalist after I sketched what I wanted. She used six shades of brown in the wings alone and Dann rigged a spotlight that comes on behind the moon at dusk. The pass-through window over my kitchen sink allows me to observe things happening in the living room and the open balcony upstairs allows a grand view of the entire downstairs.

So many people kept tabs on our progress all year and were so eager to see our green house that we held a holiday open house. Actually two open houses on two consecutive nights because we never can control guest lists. Two granddaughters helped me the first night. They answered the door and kept the food tables replenished. I chuckled when I saw those eager young faces pressed against the front door glass and one exclaimed, "Here comes another old lady!" Many guests were of our vintage, but there just weren't any old ladies. I worried about entertaining in an unfamiliar kitchen where I still can't find anything, so it's good the trial run is over. The architect who drew our plans walked around for hours delightedly listening to people's comments. The second night the two granddaughters became guests. I relieved them from working and they tore around the house with their seven cousins.

Georgiana, the woman who is restoring our old Olden homestead called looking for some of our family history. I put her off as I think my genealogy boxes are going to be the last thing unpacked.

May 1, 1995

Dear Cousins,

Today was old-fashioned May Day, but different if you're a Celt. All our Celtic friends arose before dawn dancing the sun up at Picnic Point in pagan style celebrating this quarter holiday.

We rejoiced when the court excused Dann from jury duty. He had been picked in the last 23 again and thought he'd had it until they asked if he'd ever been in court. He was there once for a traffic ticket. The next question was whether he had any negative feelings about this.

"Sure did," he replied, "because the judge didn't listen."

This broke up the entire courtroom and the judge said, "Well, I've served a lot in traffic court. I certainly hope that wasn't me!" They immediately eliminated Dann. This would have been bad timing to lose our chief carpenter, so Dann did well.

Everybody asks if we're settled, but we only look settled. Moving does not take place on one specified date. Last week we got the new dish cupboard that Dann designed and had built using old leaded windows that came out of one of our old apartments and added antique pulls and knobs to it from one of his many basement assortments. I immediately unloaded eight boxes of good dishes that I haven't used for six months. This house produces constant surprises: the beauty of the snow laden pines right outside our big windows, animal tracks cutting across the yard, the wonderful openness of the house especially the kitchen where I can now keep tabs on everything going on, my delightful green space where all my almost dead plants revived immediately after arrival, that impressive great horned owl stained glass window that hangs over the landing. Surprisingly he flies right at you when you stand in the front hall, but if you stand in the driveway outside he still swoops right at you. The full moon shines into our skylights. What a thrill and privilege it has been to design and build a house just for our wants and needs. It will truly fill the empty spot that our old 1905 farmhouse filled for so many years.

CHAPTER 30

Spider House

JUNE 12, 1995

Dear Cousins,

Moving mimics a game of lost and found. I am always looking for something that must be here. In the frenzied searching I invariably come up with what I looked for two days before. The many windows create light and sunshine but show dust quickly, my plants respond by blooming madly. We didn't throw out nearly enough stuff. I'm going to do an entire spring housecleaning to organize and move everything to where it should be, instead of where we found space to drop it.

We are leaving within the hour to spend some time with Jay. Since his divorce the kids switch every Sunday night to the other parent. Since this is Jay's week we planned around 12-year-old Allison's birthday and Gramps and I are taking her out to dinner tonight – just us three.

Andy's two youngest visited last week. They wanted to come last summer, but we firmly said not until after we moved. We took them to the Children's Museum, Ella Deli's Ice Cream Shop, attended a family party, and invited other cousins over. The highlight of the week was when we packed a picnic lunch and went to the beach. They would have settled for just that every day.

After making an effort not to travel while we were building a house, we're playing catch up. Attending an Elderhostel in the mountains of western North Carolina we learned about Scottish history taught through music, two of our favorite topics. We also enjoyed lectures on Scottish tartans, and Scottish immigration into the Appalachians. Our cabins hung on the edge of the mountain. During orientation they told us to enjoy the rocking chairs on our balconies, but if we lost anything over the rail we should call the staff.

On the same trip we took a short cruise to the Grand Bahamas as part of a promotion. Our housing was free but I don't know how families can afford to stay in that kind of luxurious living.

Traveling south through Georgia I was driving in the right hand lane of two solid lanes of traffic when a man to my left and rear apparently fell asleep at the wheel. Continuing at a forward speed he smashed into the car in front of him and then headed for the tiny space between the rear of that car and the left front of mine. As this was clearly a bad place to be, I turned the car sharply taking it off the road into the ditch, but kept in control and brought it back up again. Not far enough as he caught us anyway, but all the cars were still drivable and nobody was hurt. If our car had spun out of control and turned we would have created a mammoth pile up. Dann said he was proud of me, but I responded that I only did what anyone would have done. He replied, "No. Most people would have applied brakes."

OCTOBER 1, 1995

Dear Cousins,

Our big news is that we're going to make that trip to Australia and New Zealand. We will leave the day after tomorrow and be gone six weeks. I have been studying a lot for this trip.

I estimate that our Round Robin must be close to arriving here. I don't want it to be dead in the water for the six weeks we're gone, so I'm sending this backwards one stop. Georgiana, please add this letter and then skip me for one round.

September has been spider month. Georgiana set up a date for Dann, Andy and me to meet with the present owner of the Olden-Hibbard homestead near Pell Lake. We wanted to see how she was doing with her restoration. She wanted to pick our brains for historic tidbits. As I must have been two years old when the farm was sold out of our family, I couldn't add much. We found the house fascinating and in great shape. Dann couldn't get over how plumb the walls are after all these years. We viewed the second floor room with the sloped ceilings, where Dad and his brothers had slept. This is where my Dad (and either your Moms or your Dads) listened through the floor register while Grandmother Hibbard held spiritualist séances downstairs on the first floor. Part of one room in the basement had clearly been walled off at one time. Apparently it was made to appear as a blank wall showing no evidence of a room behind. This suggested to us that it might have contained a still or it could have been part of the Underground Railway. The house was built in the 1840s so the timing was right. Another unique thing in the basement was a vise-like contraption in the ceiling directly below the newel post that is upstairs in the front hall. It looked like that this would enable them to tighten the newel post if it loosened up. Dann woke up in the middle of the night with a different idea. The house has two front doors—one door opens to the living room and the other to the formal parlor. The parlor door was wider at one time and was probably what was called a coffin door. This tells us what the formal parlor was mostly used for. Dann surmised that the vise in the basement ceiling could loosen that newel post enough to remove it when necessary so that a coffin could be lifted and swung around into that parlor.

But back to the spider. After our concentrated study of the basement, Dann walked across the yard and felt a sting on his leg (inside his pants). He assumed he was stung by a bee although he never found any. This happened Saturday afternoon. Saturday evening we square danced. Sunday afternoon we Scottish danced. By late Sunday his leg was badly swollen. Monday morning he could hardly walk and he felt terrible. The doctor pronounced that he had cellulites probably caused by a spider bite. He put Dann on a massive dose of penicillin and Dann soon developed classic symptoms of a brown recluse spider bite. The tender spot on his leg spread into a huge, angry, ulcerated, red mass. From the knee down his leg lost all shape and his foot became swollen. Although a brown recluse bite has been known to lead to amputation, we think that the concentrated dancing on Saturday and Sunday circulated the poison throughout his system making him sicker, but saving his leg. He was confined to the couch for two weeks as walking caused extreme pain, and he suffered from bad headaches, chills, fever and nausea. Two and a half weeks passed before he could wear a shoe.

That month we oriented everything towards our blast off date. Finally things began to shape up. Dann can now walk again, our passports and visas are in order, and the rows of little slips on the pantry door, which denote places we have to go, are narrowing to a precious few. It's only when we try to leave town that we realize how many responsibilities we have thus making it a major chore to clear the slate. Letters have been flying in from Australia confirming plans, even an invitation to a Scottish dance party the day after we arrive. We keep saying we're going to travel light, but gradually books and hiking boots worked their way in. Dann needs to be properly dressed if we're going to a Scottish dance, so we added his eight-pound kilt.

We found time for a family party with all of our children and grandchildren, which doesn't happen often. We are fortunate to have a family that is close and enjoys being together. The nine cousins tore around reminding me of family parties long ago when we were the cousins tearing around. Granddaughter Allison's comment on our upcoming Australian trip was "But Grandma, you're going to miss Halloween."

CHAPTER 31

Down Under

FEBRUARY 14, 1996

Dear Cousins,

What a privilege to take a trip covering six weeks. The first two days were hopelessly complicated. On the short flight to Chicago and the three hours to L.A. the sun sank perpetually in the west, but the 12-hour leg to New Zealand in darkness was tough. Two dinners and a breakfast arrived during that long night.

I equip my travel purse with everything essential. It's my insurance should my suitcase stray. With a place for everything and everything in its place, it holds: the cribbage board and cards, a paperback novel, my journal, checkers to practice Scottish dance patterns plus direction cards for studying those dance patterns, flashlight for a night light, 57 addresses for 57 possible postcards, flight tickets and time share reservations, aspirin, Dramamine, shower cap, extra pair of glasses and eyeglass prescription, tiny screwdriver with extra glass frame screws in one end, sun glasses, collapsible sun hat, 30-power sun protection, rain bonnet, suitcase key, traveling alarm clock, miniature sewing kit, band aids with antiseptic towelettes, plastic comb, driver's license, Visa, United Mileage plus, power of attorney for health care card, directions for changing time on my watch, sizes for nine grandchildren and lots of Australian travel checks. No passport because that hangs around my neck inside my blouse where I can retrieve it quickly. No American traveler's checks because they are snuggled around my waist in a money belt, probably obliterating curves and not as invisible as I'd like to think.

We quickly established routines. The first decision was who carries what and then no deviations. My shoulder purse hung from my left shoulder across my chest and down my right side. Dann's camera bag hung on my left side keeping me balanced, but creating wide panniers on each hip so I could no longer walk down an aisle without turning sidewise. It left my hands free so I could pull my big suitcase behind and now that I have learned to pack the heavier things in the back to keep the weight down, it followed me through the airport like a well trained dog instead of a beached whale.

We left on Tuesday, but early in the morning the pilot announced that it was Thursday. Sometime during the night we had crossed the International Date Line. We collapsed when we finally reached our timeshare on the Mornington Peninsula south of Melbourne. We had moved 15 hours ahead of time at home and never did figure out what happened to Wednesday.

Our first sightseeing trip was Phillip Island to see the penguin's nightly parade. Just at dusk hundreds of tiny fairy penguins (the world's smallest penguins) stumbled out of the sea in rafts or groups hurtling themselves at the beach. They lined up like little sentinels in black and white tuxedos waiting for the stragglers to make it through the waves and undertow. It takes some of them many attempts and then they clumsily waddle across the beach and up the steep cliffs to their burrows in the sand. The day's hunt for food is over and they can return to their rookeries to feed young or rest. There are as many as 200 per acre so the wailing sounds filled the night air coming from behind every grass clump. The drive home (two hours in the dark) removed all my inhibitions about driving. Dann paid me the ultimate compliment when he promptly fell asleep as I struggled with constant oncoming lights on strange roads in an unfamiliar car and driving on the wrong side of the road. A gorgeous full moon helped illuminate the landscape and made us question "Is a full moon full the world around on the same night?"

We received an early morning phone call from a woman, identifying herself as Frances, saying she would be picking us up for the dance that night. This happened, because I had notified the RSCDS (Royal Scottish Country Dance Society) that we would be in the area. As Frances told us, "belonging to RSCDS provides instant friends." We dressed in our Scottish gear with trepidation wondering why we think we can do things like this. But when we think we can, we usually can. Frances introduced us all around to the friendly welcoming people. I managed 13 of the 14 dances. I never should have tried The Waggle of the Kilt as it had two new movements I couldn't assimilate. Dann's leg was swollen again that night after dancing and even though it was late, we filled our tub with steaming water, turned on the jets and soaked for a long time.

It impresses me when we travel at how visible American life is worldwide. When in England it was the Falklands and why didn't our president do something? Here it was O.J. Simpson and how can we allow something like that to happen? I cringe at the image we portray. I felt better when the conversation switched to the problems of the Aborigines that sound just like the problems of our Native Americans. This was a great opportunity to explore Australian minds. We feel like we've been adopted by the Scots on this peninsula. We had invitations to go dancing every night, but have passed them up in an effort to give Dann's leg a chance to heal so he can dance again when we reach Canberra, the nation's capital.

While on the southern coast we chose to explore the Great Ocean Road that stretches west for 200 miles. We crossed the bay by ferry. As the Ocean Road stretched farther than we could go in one day, we had to catch the first ferry across and the last one back. I carefully clocked our driving time allowing time for photo stops and tea. We are already addicted to their specialties and cheerfully munched our way through fish and chips, sausage rolls, chocolate truffle cakes, Devonshire tea (with scones, cream and jam) and cappuccino. Passing spectacular scenery as the twisty road crept along the side of the mountains with waves crashing far below; we occasionally descended to sea level. If we missed that last ferry we would have a three hour drive around the bay, but we arrived back at the wharf with an hour to spare.

Every trip has some narrow escapes. As we loaded onto the ferry I stepped out, locked my side of the car and Dann did likewise. As I started for the stairs I heard him exclaim "Oh, no." Turning I saw a dismayed look on his face and instantly realized we had both locked our doors with the keys in the ignition. We still had fifteen minutes before departure so Dann went for help coming back with a crewman and two long wires. Each man took one side of the car and silently went to work. Fifteen minutes passed. The ramp came up. The ferry pushed off. This was a short ferry ride giving Dann only 40 minutes to work. The car brakes were on so only a tow could move us off. It was the last eastbound ferry of the day. There was one more westbound that would take us back and leave us stranded on the wrong side of the bay for the night. Dann gave up on the wire when he discovered the back window would move one-quarter inch. A line of spectators formed on the railing above. Dann wiggled his window down an inch and rocked it by placing his palms flat on the glass and alternately pushing up and down over and over. As the eastern shore approached, the glass slipped three inches, just enough for a hand to reach in. I thanked the attendant, but he replied, "Thank your husband. He was the expert."

We studied Australian history in the capital and joined more Scottish dancers. On those long, busy days Dann's leg would swell by nightfall. I would wrap it in hot towels while he elevated it during our evening cribbage.

We attended the *Marriage of Figaro* at the beautiful opera house in Sydney. Just outside the opera house swarms of sailboats on the harbor skimmed the water and strong winds filled colorful spinnakers. Here in Sydney, our last year's Friendship Force guest picked us up. He drove us north on the Pacific Highway, a gorgeous stretch of road meandering between sandstone outcroppings, rolling hills, through forests of gum trees and past sandy beaches, always with the Dividing Range to the west and the Pacific Ocean on the east. Huge Norfolk Island pines stood sentinel guard and balls of bougainvillea blooms dotted the coast.

Our ultimate destination was the Barrier Reefs. I took a twelve hour seasickness pill, but they insisted that Dann also take a Travel aid. This was my first alert for trouble ahead. We sailed aboard a beautiful two-story catamaran and as we neared the mouth of the river approaching the open sea I chose my spot carefully – upstairs, near an open window. Within ten minutes I gratefully used the bags conveniently placed nearby. Dann told me afterward that people were stretched out all over the floor. Wind speed at 15 knots created enormous swells. The trip out to Lady Musgrave Island took two and one-half hours. All I could think of was those poor immigrants crossing this "bloody" ocean. Immediately upon arrival the captain announced that the semi-submersible was waiting alongside. I stumbled aboard wondering how long it would take before I even cared. This craft lowered us six feet into the water and we cruised around the edges of the reef. Constant narration identified coral and fish. Shoals, islands and 2,500 individual coral reefs stretch across an area larger than the British Isles buffering northeastern Queensland from the pounding surf of the Pacific. This reef is the largest living structure on earth and was declared a marine park in 1975. After a sumptuous buffet lunch we took the glass-bottomed boat to explore Lady Musgrave Island and then returning we swam around the catamaran to cool off. This small coral island is the only one on the reef with a navigable lagoon. As we left, the captain had to steer through a narrow neck of water, make a sharp 90 degree left turn and then turn due east between two reefs for some time before he could turn west and head for home. I wasn't sure I wanted to go home if I had to sail on that catamaran again, but the skies were blue and sunny allowing us to search for whales, but saw none.

It was a great three weeks in Australia—except for the Wednesday that we lost. We were handed from new friend to new friend starting with Frances who picked us up for our first RSCDS dance and invited us home for steak; Beryl and Rich who drove us to the mountains for the day; Allison who met our plane in Canberra and drove us to dance class, to our Evergreen Bed & Breakfast host in Sydney who met us at the Rail station; to Ern who picked us up in Sydney and drove us 600 miles up the coast.

Australia has some unique things: no tipping, electric teakettles with instant coffee and tea in every motel room, toilets that give a choice of a half flush or total flush, all kinds of takeout food, overtaking lanes that make passing a snap, something called pumpkin that tastes like squash, lush flowers everywhere and a growing season twelve months of the year. Some things are not so good: $2.00 and $1.00 coins means that you're carrying heavy change, dangerous showers where the hot and cold are on the wrong side and sometimes turn the wrong way, revolving doors and buffet lines that work backwards, atmosphere that requires a sun hat even when cloudy and pokies (slot machines) all over. We saw much, but in three weeks saw only a small bit of Australia.

Each day of exploration challenged us. We flew to Auckland on New Zealand's North Island and my watch lost three hours. This land of the Maoris enthralled us as we headed far north to the famous Bay of Islands. According to Maori legend, the first Polynesian explorer visited this bay in the tenth century. We hopped on a Wave rider tour bus—an eleven-hour trip to the far north with a non-stop narrative by our Scottish driver. Everything in the Northland has Maori impossible-to-pronounce, sound-alike names but Alex, our driver, rolled them off effortlessly. Cone-shaped peaks covered with green pasture over fertile soil dot this ancient volcanic land of mountainous terrain. Mature kauri trees rival redwoods in age, height, and girth and can be 2,000 years old.

Driving through gorges the road often makes 128 degree turns, always up or down or around a curve and we passed masses of wild nasturtiums, pampas grass, and solid fields of Arum lilies running rampant along the roadsides. Flame trees blazed with masses of blossoms. As we walked through the Glo-worm cave a thousand sparkles of light on the ceiling from the hanging larvae penetrated the cave darkness. We inspected the yard where the huge swamp Kauri trees, buried underground for 30,000 years, are being retrieved to make spectacular furniture. Travelling to Cape Reinga, New Zealand's most northern point, supposed to be the departing place of the Maori spirits, we looked down through swirling mist where the two oceans meet—Tasman on the west and the Pacific on the east.

The climax of the day came as we anticipated the Sixty-Mile Beach. Alex was a wee bit concerned because that night would be full moon, which means high tide, and he needed lower tide to safely drive on the beach. The only access from the north was through the TePaki quicksand stream. Alex drove through it rapidly. Two turns downstream took us onto the beach where white breakers crashed as far as we could see. Alex drove into the ocean and swung into several tight donuts before stopping back on the sand beach. "Just testing" he said and then waited 15 minutes for the tide to recede. Two buses and two mini-buses arrived, zoomed around, conferred with Alex and departed. But we waited and left last.

Driving the beach is an art. Alex judges by the color of the sand and stays just below the wave line avoiding the light-colored soft sand and hoping no big waves rock us. Speed is important to prevent bogging down. No one stops. As our bus was the biggest and heaviest we also went the fastest and bypassed everyone splashing spray from our wheels. We swayed back and forth. If extra large waves approached Alex downshifted and slowed. We passed a half-sunken vehicle that had been there two weeks and would vanish in another three. No residents drive on this beach, only dumb tourists. Last year, 17 cars were lost to the sand and no insurance covers that.

Blasting off the beach through another creek bed, Alex drove the bus over a cement square where jet sprays from below washed the sand from its belly. We replenished our nerves with tea, reluctantly abandoned the ancient land of the Maoris and flew to Christchurch on the South Island.

We must have seen most of New Zealand's sixty million sheep as we traveled south. In Dunedin we caught up with more Scottish dancers. Some of these dances, like Mairi's wedding, were familiar to us and when I commented afterwards to Peggy, the teacher, that in Wisconsin we put in an extra twirl on that dance she responded, "Yes, that makes it a dizzy dance. Please don't mention that. I dinna want to stir the purridge ennymore. "

After crossing the continent to the west coast and viewing the famous Milford Sound in the rain we stopped for a week's rest and reorganization at our time share in Wanaka. One day we drove to Queenstown and Lake Wakatipu and took the coal-burning steamer across the lake to a high country sheep station. Joey, the sheep dog; brought Robbie, the Scottish Highland bull, up from the back paddock. This station keeps 20,000 sheep. Two weeks ago they brought the flock down for muster and this took three men, eighteen dogs and twelve days. After shearing, the sheep are protected in a lower pasture for a week, given extra feed and then turned loose to work their way back up.

Daylight lingered, and because we didn't have to hurry and weren't tired, we took the short route over the Crown Range back to our time share. The shortcut we had been advised not to take home. The Alpine Crown Range road is a scenic alternative to Highway 6 going from Wanaka to Queenstown, a 44-mile route closed in winter, not recommended for nervous drivers. The first thing that meets your eye is the "No caravan" sign, after which the road, laid out like a Z, immediately moves steeply up the mountainside. Unbelievably tight, steeply graded turns offered no visibility around the bend. Soon we towered high above Queenstown, the valley and the lake. The sealed road ceased and we continued on corrugated gravel. I hesitantly asked, "You wouldn't consider turning around, would you?"

"No way," Dann countered, "would I think of going down that road we just came up." Although I thought we were all the way up, we were not. We continued gradually winding upward around mountain after mountain until we could see the entire Wakatipu Valley far below. At 3,675 feet above sea level this is the highest road in New Zealand. It also must have been the most twisted and narrowest as we often used the entire road going around blind curves. Eventually we trailed down alongside a dancing stream as we wound between mountains. The blacktop returned and the clouds hanging around the mountaintops hung no more. We drove home the same way we had left—in pouring rain. With one difference, we agreed to no more driving on unsealed roads.

With time to spare the next day we explored the road that wound around our side of Lake Wanaka. We drove only a mile when the sealed road deteriorated into corrugated gravel, accompanied by a sign that warned "Proceeding on this road might be hazardous to your health." We had already agreed to turn around instantly whenever blacktop gave out and no longer needed a warning sign. Both life and New Zealand are full of shortcuts, some unwise and some time-consuming.

We arrived in Madison at 7:35 p.m. five minutes after we had left New Zealand. I had waited for this ever since the day we had lost Wednesday en route. When we crossed the International Date Line we picked up Monday twice. So we were even.

CHAPTER 32

Home Sweet Home

APRIL 2, 1996

Dear Cousins,

It's good to be home. I have created a long "honey do" list for Dann during these winter months. The basement tops the list. In the pressure of moving, we just dumped many boxes in the basement and now Dann has to organize his shop before he can unpack. Spending more time writing still sits at the top of my list. It's tough to give it first priority, but sometimes the top of my list is the only one that makes it. In addition to my monthly column for Dane Co. Kids, I have accepted the position of Dane County president for Extension Homemakers and this involves a monthly newsletter. Enrolling in the writing class again means a weekly assignment and all that makes a life of deadlines. I enjoy the writing, but wish I could just roll it off without so much thinking. I threaten to write in the middle of the night to avoid the continual phone interruptions which take my thinking off track.

My president's job for Extension Homemakers keeps me busy and I try to emulate what we called a "rocking chair Scoutmaster." That occurred when Dann, as Cubmaster, assigned all the jobs and then relaxed—just checking on them occasionally. I began by filling all the vacancies on the executive board and instigated a program of calling to remind people of the board meetings telling them the president couldn't do this by herself. I hated it when the last president held meetings and only a few attended and I proudly tallied 100% at my last meeting.

We finally found our cross-country skis and discovered that we can strap them on outside our back door, ski through the gate in our board fence onto a groomed cross country trail in the park. I believe this will mean more company. For the last two Sundays, a son and granddaughter came for lunch and to ski.

Dann has many slides from our down under trip so we worked out a slide show accompanied by script and music and held an open house. This coincided with a granddaddy of a blizzard and we couldn't cancel because we didn't know who was coming. Many who came got stuck a block away.

In an effort to spend extra time with Jay's family this year, we try to visit once a month in spite of the weather. We went for Trevor's birthday and did a request performance for his class. They have been studying the Pacific and will be working on Australia, Hawaii and Alaska. We found slides for all three. Trevor is in a four, five and six grade team class. I thought we would be addressing about 25, but combination grades are team teachers. The other three teachers were also interested, so we addressed 100 kids for an hour. Dann ran the projector while I talked. Keeping that many seated on the floor and quiet for an hour is usually impossible, but they were great. They asked so many good questions that we could hardly get away.

We'll be doing this again next week for Michelle's class. This presentation will be on Uzbekistan for a normal size class, making me realize how much I miss the school forest kids. It also makes me realize grandparents are important.

Dann's leg still swells from that spider bite when he dances a lot. We realize how lucky we were it wasn't worse although it was awful at the time. Expressing myself in this letter is cathartic making me observe details in my daily life. I believe life was designed to be full of ups and downs, fraught with challenges. Each day facing multitudinous problems and sometimes failures I often go to bed feeling that nothing worked right that day, but each morning I'm ready to climb the mountains again.

Yes, I know what calamari is, but I ate it for a week before anyone told me.

I cannot believe that my cousin asks her mailman to wait while she finishes her Round Robin letter. Actually we've been inviting ours in for hot coffee because the chill factor has been -30 degrees.

June 1, 1996

Dear Cousins,

I labeled this grandparents' spring. After we traveled to Minnesota and gave that program on Australia to Trevor's 4-5-6 grade they were so pleased that they set up a World Culture Week. They invited parents who had traveled and would share their experiences to come for an hour during that week. They issued Dann and me a special invitation to come back and do Scotland. We wore our formal Scottish dress. I took a long piece of woolen yardage; hand folded it into pleats, laid it on the floor on top of a belt, chose a boy to lie down and belted it around him to show how the original great kilts were used. Demonstrating how to throw the extra end around his head to make a hood I also tied it around his waist to make a pocket. We told some gory history stories, taught the girls to curtsey and the boys to bow, and asked for volunteers to demonstrate a wee bit of dancing – difficult when one has 100 kids in an average-size classroom. Their World Culture week consisted of three periods per day and they studied three different countries concurrently, so the entire school participated. The kindergarten and first graders joined in by bringing samples of ethnic food for the tasting fair. By drawing on the expertise of parents or grandparents that school has created a fantastic program. For us to deal with 100 well behaved children amazes me.

Next we visited Michelle's 6th grade this spring and did a program on Uzbekistan. Our grandparent participation shifted to sports when we visited Delavan to watch Tony run on the Varsity track team. This required sitting on bleachers in arctic winds for two hours before he ran. Next, we went to Verona to watch Luke's baseball game and froze again. Grandma business is hard work. I can see I am going to need long johns again. I had thought I was past that.

In between grandkids we've been dancing lots. We barely recovered from our annual Scottish Ball before attending the Iowa Ball, more hours of dancing. After the ball, the musicians played—improvising as they went. Dann was put out when I insisted that we leave at 2:00 a.m. and go to bed as we had to drive home the next day.

SEPTEMBER 11, 1996

Dear Cousins,

Yesterday Dann and I got up at 5:00 a.m. and wondered why we still work at the polls. Madison has changed from the old voting machines. Now that we're computerized it's easier to close at night. Getting home by 9:00 p.m. meant that we had only worked 15 hours instead of the 16-17 that we used to. People don't like to change and we get a lot of moans and groans about wanting to go back to the old system. However, now when we close at 8:00 p.m. we push a "print tape' button and the computer rolls everything out.

Those old machines frequently broke down. On the last presidential election I called for help three times in one hour for the same machine. As the repair lady went out the door the third time she muttered, "I have other people to take care of. If that one breaks down again just roll it out in the street in front of the largest truck you can find."

People need to complain if they've been standing too long in line and who is more convenient than the election workers? We've learned to grin and tell them, "Sorry, but these new machines really are more efficient."

So, don't forget to vote in November. Expect to stand in line and please smile at the tired people behind the table. If you can't suffer the lines a presidential election will always have, use an absentee ballot. Sorry about the lecture. I had to be nice yesterday. Today I get to say what I think.

When a summer cottage, such as ours, is owned by multiple owners, maintenance requires organization. That means a work weekend with many people and this year we organized a great one. With an array of necessary jobs, I had horrible visions of everything getting half done when it was time to leave, visions of a diminished work crew as conflicts crowded in on people's weekend, and expectations of terrible weather when we needed to work outside. None of this happened. Willett's all over the place completed every job and the weather was delightful. Dann counted 12 people working on the roof. I accused him of miscounting as there was much too much movement on the roof to get an accurate count. Two highpoints of the weekend were the beautiful clear water coming from the kitchen faucet because they had installed a bladder tank and the impressive number of fourth generation Willett's involved. Most everyone worked at ripping off the old roof and pulling nails—even seven-year-old Aaron and nine-year-old George were allowed to help. The men started roofing on the lake side and a second crew started on the kitchen side and both crews worked simultaneously toward the ridgepole. The four teenage second cousins, Tony, Ben, Shaun and Nicky, made quite a team. They carried and loaded the entire gunk into two utility trailers and then reversed the process at the Iron River dump. They stripped saplings to make a new railing and to use as erosion logs across the trail. Finally they took out the dock and after everybody else dropped into bed exhausted, the four second cousins built a beach fire and sat around visiting.

The chimney was straightened and enlarged so it could operate more efficiently, necessitating much cleaning as stuff had filtered through into the room. Although it was late in the season, some brave souls took dips in the lake. I heard many comments of stiffness and aching muscles on Sunday. Because people were constantly moving it was hard to take a count but I estimated 4 second generation, 11 third generation and 12 fourth generation. This cottage planned and built by A.D. Willett continues to bond this family.

The North American Manx convention was held in Madison this year. The Isle of Man lies in the Irish Sea midway between Ireland and England. Dann's grandmother was one of the Manx who immigrated to Wisconsin. Our state society meets twice a year, but the National Association has conventions bi-annually.

Dann and I were in charge of the music and dance. We arranged three hours of a Celtic dancing performance at the Saturday Farmer's Market on the Square. Twenty of our Scottish dancers performed with a bagpiper, who put out so much volume that it drew people from the far side of the Square. Spectators sat on the grass and listened.

We set up a similar demonstration for the next day at Pendarvis Historical site in Mineral Point. I volunteered to arrange bus schedules and serve as a tour guide on the lead bus from Madison to Mineral Point and planned a historical and natural history itinerary. People on the bus peppered me with questions. Starting in Madison in glaciated land, we crossed terminal moraines into the famous drift less area of southwestern Wisconsin and Wisconsin's unique geology. One man stopped as he got off the bus and told me, "I am a geologist. My ears perked up when you started talking, but you got it all perfect even correct terms and pronunciation." I didn't know in advance that I had a geologist aboard. This made me realize again how much I miss teaching my School Forest kids.

I soon learned, that weekend, not to worry about things that weren't my problem such as: the harpist from London who hadn't arrived one hour prior to her concert, or the nail in Dann's tire that he drove around with because he had no time to change it, or whether Dann was keeping the Cornish pasties hot and the salads cold for the picnic supper we provided for the dancers. I worried about keeping my buses on schedule and learned that when I was dancing I can't think about anything else, or my feet go in the wrong direction. I learned that I am not a head table person where I can't visit and have to stay awake. It was more fun sitting at other tables where we made new friends.

Every day we worried because we had not yet sold the Old Sauk Road house. To claim the one-time tax exemption requires that we live in that dwelling as primary residence for three of the last five years and our time is running out in November of this year.

No thanks Dorothy. I would not like you to volunteer me for the Racine schools. I have more than I can handle with the schools of nine grandchildren.

Fran, what did you mean when you said the injury Grandfather Elijah received in the Civil War eventually took his life? What did Grandpa die of?

December 3, 1996

Dear Cousins,

Thanksgiving has traditionally been at our house. We can still entertain in this house, but have to plan differently with less space. When Jay comes from Minnesota with three kids all the other cousins immediately zero in. First Martha asked to come for overnight, then Michelle and finally Luke. I gave up and asked the rest too. "Just bring your sleeping bags," I told them, "because the adults have claimed all the beds." We had a total of 24.

We took the kids to the YMCA pool to use up their excess energy. The two little girls started counting owls in Grandma Owl's house, quickly reaching 50. When the adults arose in the morning, the girls could search those bedrooms too and reached 84. By the time they went home they had found 102. This game took hours. Pictures on the wall were easy, but soon they discovered potholders, candles, fireplace andirons, embroidery on the bedspread, plant hangers, stained glass window, pillows, scatter rugs and on and on. They never tired of searching.

Our big news is that we have finally sold our old house. We tried frantically all summer as son Andy, our CPA, kept prodding us. We bought it 40 years ago and really needed that one-time exemption for capital gains. We thought of creative ideas such as moving back, or one of us moving back, or selling it to the kids, but couldn't do that legally. We had to have an offer with a closing date before November 8. Late in September we made moves to rent it and reclassify as a business rental property. We put a "For Rent" ad in the paper, but also placed a "For Sale" ad. On October 8, we received an offer—not one that we were happy with as this is an ideal family house with its five bedrooms and we sold it to a bachelor. We suspect he may tear it down and subdivide, but could not concern ourselves with that. Time was of the essence for the closing date and we were able to close in one week. For two years friends have asked if I didn't miss the old house and I didn't. We enjoyed all the special things in our new house and besides we still went back to the old one. We took our dance class there because that long empty expanse of wooden floors was ideal for practicing set dances. I lugged pails of prime dirt from my compost bed there to my flower beds here and found wildflowers in the woods that I had transplanted once and I transplanted again. All that changed on the last afternoon when Dann and I walked through the entire acre and through every room including the attic and basement and locked the door behind us. Each room and each tree brought back memories because the nostalgia gets greater when we can't go back anymore. This is a great relief. Taking care of one house is enough. Caring for two was difficult.

 I have been doing piano-organ duets. I did this several times with the church organist and then tried a new angle telling our 16-year-old grandson what I'd really like for a Christmas present would be for him to play a duet with me in church and he said, "Okay." Luke plays well, but hasn't had experience performing and neither have I on the organ which makes this a challenge with two nervous people shaking on their piano benches.

 Once more we survived deer season, but five deer didn't survive the Willett's. We have friends with a weekend farmhouse in heavily wooded western Wisconsin who loan it to the Willett's for hunting weekend. This means that when the weather gets lousy, which it usually does, the humans stay dry and warm. It enables them to eat well because the kitchen has an old wood stove. This weekend includes three generations of Willett's who have a great time just being together. The first couple of years our grandsons were allowed only to walk alongside their fathers, but now after a gun safety course two of them are shooting. This year, one granddaughter asked to go. This perturbed Dann as there is only one bed, which he gets by seniority, and he wondered if he was going to lose it. I told him, "No way. She can sleep on the floor with the rest." He did wonder how this was going to work as nobody but he had ever worn pajamas. But it worked.

This year both of us danced with the demo team for the Ethnic Festival. It is scary to walk out on the big stage ringed with spotlights so you can't see the audience. Maybe that's good. Both of us had to memorize six dances, but that's not good enough. Inevitably there comes a point when one's mind blanks out momentarily and one hopes that the person next to you will give a slight tug. This performing is gratifying—after you're finished.

I am putting in lots of time as county president for the Homemakers. I'd rather be writing or traveling, but I owe it to the organization as I've learned so much from our lessons over the years. I've surprised many of my board members as I start my meetings at 7:00 p.m. and quit two hours later no matter what. At 7:00 I hand out a single red carnation to anyone who did something I especially appreciated. That shakes them up. The first carnation went to the woman who lives at the far corner of the county and drove 60 miles round trip to attend the meeting. We are promoting a sewing project in Nicaragua. The Madison/Nicaragua partnership has established sewing clinics there and has supplied us with a long list of needed supplies. Most of my Homemakers were seamstresses at one time and still, like me, have closets full of stuff too good to throw away. The first time I asked for donations I filled 12 bushel size boxes with material, needles, pins, scissors, used zippers and whatever. The second time I asked, I filled 29. The Nicaraguan women are being taught to make their own clothes and how to sew for profit.

Fran, your comments about Grandpa Hibbard were extremely interesting. I can't understand how that wound would cause trouble so many years later. Is it possible that it never healed?

When I called our 13-year-old granddaughter yesterday, she signed off with "see you later" and I've been enjoying that thought. What a delightful way to terminate a conversation. So I say to all of you "see you later". It may take awhile before we meet again so hold on to that thought.

Jean Hibbard Willett

FEBRUARY 3, 1997

Dear Cousins,

As you read this letter you all may realize that we finally got that new computer with a magnificent new printer. All my committee people are breathing sighs of relief that they can read what I've sent. The flip side is that this Gateway 2000, 133 Pentium is the fastest way to reduce one's self-confidence. It's a mystery to me in areas that I need desperately to use. When it arrived, Andy installed it, rapidly showed me a couple things and said, "Now read the manual." I needed some things done right away and didn't have time to study. Instead I used the sink or swim method and tried all the buttons. There seems to be an elaborate filing system like the branches of a tree. Not understanding how to move from here to there I scattered my eggs all over the barnyard making this a hide and seek game. One day I typed an article for a newsletter and filed it somewhere. Later I hunted for half an hour to find it and decided as I had a deadline it would be quicker to write it over. The next day the original turned up where it should never have gone. I have now mastered writing letters, which includes editing, saving and printing. I can play Monopoly, Hearts or solitaire. I can play our CD's (even turn down the volume) and can read the dictionary. I have yet to master the bookkeeping systems, making greeting cards, access the Mayo Clinic health line or the World Wide Web. Every other night I come to the supper table frustrated enough to shut the blasted thing off and give up. On the few good nights I am exhilarated at the possibilities this offers and have a hard time even stopping to cook. This is an exciting age we live in although it would have been easier to stay computer illiterate as others of my age have done.

I made a New Year's resolution to spend more time with my grandchildren. This is compatible with my intense desire to conquer this computer. Just ask the kids to show you how something works as even the little ones run circles around me. I

Dear Cousins

bought myself a book called WINDOWS 95 FOR DUMMIES. That should help.

No, Dorothy, this is NOT a short letter. I just haven't learned how to enlarge this small print.

CHAPTER 33

Graduation Month

JULY 3, 1997

Dear Cousins,

Summers fill up with grandchildren. We took our oldest grandson to Quebec City for a week for his high school graduation present. Realizing that Quebec is French-speaking, we depended on Tony's years of conversational French to keep us out of hot water. This experiment turned out great and we worked constantly on our French vocabulary. Tony would say *oui* or *merci* and then walk out of the store quickly before they could ask him questions. Dann would throw around his few choice phrases such as *merci beaucoup* and *s'il vous plait* putting him in bad trouble when some responded in rapid French. Stopping first at a gas station we were forced to ascertain the difference between *avec service* and *libre service*. We managed in restaurants where one can point, but learned that entrée in this country gets you only appetizers. Dann and Tony ordered sandwiches. I thought we should expand our tastes and vocabulary and pointed to a special I could neither read nor pronounce. We made a deal to share whatever came. My first course, *pate,* arrived on a large plate containing a few scraggly pieces of watercress, cucumbers, small tomato, and two tiny pieces of sliced meat. Dann and Tony declined to sample this. A tossed salad followed. Again they declined. The third course, *chocolait gateau* covered with hot fudge sauce, everybody shared enthusiastically.

Tony tried to teach us to count with his limit of 20. Each night he added another number or two: *un, deux, trios, quatre, cinq, sets, sept, huift* . . . When he got to *quatorze*, our week was up. I searched in vain for a bakery all week and learned on the last day that the *boulangierre* was just across the street.

I stipulated that we explore historic old Quebec the first day and by the end of that day Tony was addicted, as I am, to history. In spite of intense heat and hundreds of steps up to reach Old Town, we retraced our steps three times. Tony has always had trouble reading. History presented in three dimensions and stereophonically with rifles firing behind us kept him spellbound. As he had never seen an ocean we drove up the St. Laurence looking for whales, who didn't cooperate. We showed him tidal water in action and explored several stupendous waterfalls. As we walked through the nature trails Dann commented that going into the woods with a track team grandchild simulates taking a dog for a walk—he covers thrice the distance we do, but comes back to check on us occasionally. That beautiful countryside reminded me of our North Woods.

Evening routine, when we were hot and exhausted, consisted of splashing in the pool, cooking supper, Tony and Gramps matched at Cribbage, three-way Spite and Malice, journal writing and a struggle through French-speaking movies. Bedtime arrived when we couldn't stand the frustration of watching without interpretation. We tried to provide Tony with a lifetime memory and we succeeded. This starts an intriguing tradition, but Dann thinks we'll never make it through nine grandchildren.

New France left us with vivid impressions: the natural beauty as it perches between the mountains and the St. Lawrence River and their history that precedes ours with continual struggles to survive with scurvy, influenza, smallpox, diphtheria, frequent wars and daily threats of devastating fires and floods. Through it all they persevered. Old churches dominate every village and cathedrals grace every city reflecting the significance of religion on those early settlers. Constantly struggling to listen and interpret we discovered that body language helped. Everyone tried to understand us as exemplified by the girl at the black currant winery. "*Au revoir et merci beaucomp*," I told her as I went out the door.

She grinned and replied, "Good-bye and you're welcome."

Four days before leaving for Quebec our company from Australia had turned up in Madison earlier than expected. Ritchie was one of the Scottish dancers who had showed us wonderful hospitality when we were in Melbourne and he is now touring the United States by bicycle. Landing in Seattle he allotted four months to bike from the west coast to the east coast—an undertaking at age 72. We enjoyed having him for four days. Unfortunately I was attending College Days for Women on campus, but Dann took him to the House on the Rock, Farmers' Market, Veterans' Museum, the Dependable Auto Body (Mike's shop) and all the bike shops in town. At one of the shops he bought a new improved bike. We took him along to Tony's graduation because he said he'd like to see an American graduation ceremony, but after sitting for three hours on the top bleacher in intense heat he commented, "Well, I don't need to do that again." As this overlapped with our Quebec trip we left him in possession of the house. He wanted to stay one more day so he could dance with our Scottish dancers on Sunday night.

Don (Dann's brother) and Ritchie drove us across town to the airport. Don then took Ritchie home for a "cuppa" before delivering him to Mike and Susie. She found them curb seats to watch Verona's annual parade. Mike runs the Chamber of Commerce float and he's the only one who can keep that float running. They took him home for lunch before returning him to our house by the designated time, where Scottish dancers picked him up, took him out for supper and to dance class. Other dancers took him to their house afterwards for a "cuppa" and returned him again to our house. Monday morning he closed the house and continued trekking eastward. I was proud of my remote control arrangements, but disappointed that we couldn't dance with him once more. He allowed four months to bike from Seattle to Boston, but he made it in three.

The College Week for Women on the University campus kept me busy that week. Every morning I attended three hours of concentrated computer training. Two teachers, wandering around behind us, would help when we got submerged in trouble—not if, but when. I managed many bad things like freezing my machine, losing my memory, getting stuck in the advertising and generally getting lost as I wandered around in search engines. Fabulous material lurks there for genealogists. I just need time to pursue it.

    I have finished the main bulk of my *Dear Mom* book. I ultimately decided that unless I said NO to everything that I didn't have to do that I would never finish the writing. I have edited it four times, read it aloud to Dann, sent it to my writing instructor and now am busy checking her editing. I've worked on this for many years, but am now reaching that scary point where I'm not sure what's next.

NOVEMBER 3. 1997

Dear Cousins,

    Visiting grandchildren again filled much of this last summer. Wearily I have decided grandparents ARE important. We asked to have one of Jay's kids for half a week and instead got all three for a full week. The one who lives in Madison wanted to see her cousins, of course, so she moved in Monday morning and stayed also. Because I simply can't handle all our summer birthdays I set up a Willett family birthday potluck and covered everybody May through September. Allison, aged 14, made a double cake in my 13-inch pan and with 13-year-old Michelle's help, spent all day decorating. This included writing Happy Birthday and 23 names around the top and it didn't take me too long to get the purple frosting off the walls. We would make lunch and then depart for the beach every morning. Once we persuaded Gramps to take a two-hour lunch hour and join us. We played cards continually. One night all the cousins went to their Uncle Tim's for a pizza sleepover that allowed Grandpa and Grandma Owl a needed rest. Tim said that he laid out sleeping bags like cordwood on the living room floor and Tim's two year-old step-grandchild, with great delight, jumped up and down on the sleeping bags periodically throughout the night. We took the three Minnesotans back on Friday stopping at the Circus World Museum in Baraboo en route.

The Scottish dancers are again practicing for the Ethnic Festival. Last summer we started a Scot-Kids group who will join us for one dance so eight-year-old Martha will be performing on stage with us. Two weeks ago I reached into the oven when I shouldn't have and I've been dancing with only one hand since. My knuckles are swollen and my fingers red and tender to the touch. I wrapped that hand in bandages to warn my partners not to grab. Instead of putting my hand out to grasp I held it up so they grabbed my wrist instead. This takes two extra seconds and throws off our timing.

Georgiana, we were impressed with your grandson's funeral. I chuckled over his father's shoes under the coffin when I realized that George had declared, because his son had never wanted to wear shoes and was not being buried in shoes, that as his father, he wasn't going to wear shoes that day either. Car accidents happen so quickly and when younger loved ones are taken this greatly increases the tragedy.

Georgiana, I have been trying to decide who gets to sample the big Chinook that we caught when fishing with you on Lake Michigan. Tim has made enough pointed remarks that I think his family, and Mike's, are slated for fish dinner next Monday. He has requested a place on that boat to qualify as two years worth of birthday presents.

Go for getting a computer, Lorraine. It's absolutely wonderful what one can do—when it's working. When it's not, it convinces me that I am the dumbest person alive. Fortunately I have sons to bail me out.

CHAPTER 34

School in Ireland

January 5, 1998

Dear Cousins,

We finally gambled on an overseas Elderhostel and signed up for Ireland. I never feel like we're going away until that airplane door slams behind us, especially when traveling with dangerous Dann who, without warning, pulls stunts like waking up unable to walk a straight line 24 hours prior to take-off. We rushed him to emergency and they ruled out all the horrifying possibilities and diagnosed it as an inner ear infection that might be better in 48 hours. But Dann has a high survival tolerance and doused with medication by boarding time, he could walk on board without staggering.

Flying Boston to Shannon was a long trip, but a short night. Supper remains weren't cleared until 11:00 p.m., but at 1:30 a.m. they turned the lights back on and appeared with breakfast. We zipped through landing procedures through to the Arrival Hall where our Elderhostel shepherd waited. After an hour's drive through the countryside, we arrived at Belinter House, an old country estate now a conference center. It stands on the bank of the Boyne River, a river that follows the history of Ireland. Belinter, a Georgian mansion, was designed in 1750 for the grandfather of the first Lord Tara. We reached the second floor, reserved for family life, by using the graceful, narrow, steep circular stairway that curved up from the front hall.

With the kitchens located in the west wing, it must have been difficult for the servants to keep the food warm on its long journey through the basement and up that spiral staircase. One of the early owners, after wining and dining extremely well one evening, rode his horse up that staircase on a wager. He won. However, after ascending to the top the horse refused to come down and remained in the attic for three weeks until they could erect a beam and pulley that lowered the horse to ground level.

Every morning we attended lectures on Irish art or history. Every afternoon the bus took us on field trips. Mike, the driver, handled that coach with expertise as he rolled down narrow country roads with built-up sides and high hedges. We chugged up curvy mountain roads and over passes, viewed old monasteries and traveled 5,000 years back in time to view Tara Hill, the seat of the priest-kings before written history. One day we headed for New Grange, a prehistoric passage grave. Coming home on narrow back roads, Michael did a great job of handling our large coach until we met a black VMW that stopped both of us. A huge Irishman piled out of the VMW loudly demanding "Where do ye expect me ta go?" Our on-site coordinator stuck her head out an open window and when he spotted her he hesitated and sputtered, "Oh, is that you, Maura and how are ye?"

"Now," she asked, "how am I going to explain to a bus load of Americans that an Irishman doesn't know any better than to drive a big VMW on a back road? We'll do the best we can for ye Patrick, but yer just gonna have to back up." He looked ready to blast us off the road. Maura said that he doesn't back down for anybody, but he did, along with the four cars now stuck behind him. Maura did not direct our coach down that back road again.

After a week we traveled across Ireland to the University of Limerick campus. We moved from the life of a noble county gentleman to that of a student in a modern community. A van delivered a catered breakfast to our common room every morning and we ate lunch in the campus cafeteria. I thought this was good until I discovered they sneaked rutabagas, which I detest, into the chili. Morning lectures covered traditional Irish music. Afternoon field trips, often north into county Clare, took us into pubs as we searched for the heart of traditional Irish music.

Dear Cousins

All trips have drudgery days, but when one travels in a group humdrum things become easier. We only had to set bags outside the door and they were taken to the airport. Our coach delivered us to Shannon where we parted company with our new friends and took off on our own for Somerset, Devon and Cornwall.

We fell in love with the unique, often isolated, Bed and Breakfasts and with the strange moors. We drove out on the Bodmin Moor to the Jamaica Inn where I wanted to stay. The Jamaica Inn was built in 1547 as a residence, then used as a temperance house and finally as an inn. The sign over the door reads "Smugglers, wreckers, villains and thieves entered here long ago." We walked on the cobbled courtyard over which stage coaches had rattled, and listened to the swinging sign creaking in the breeze. We stayed in the room named Josh that provided great atmosphere by loud creaking of the floors whenever we walked and learned all about the author when we visited the Daphne du Maurer museum.

We traveled down the west coast of Devon and Cornwall to Land's End and then back up the east coast. We saw antiquities and learned Celtic history including the Arthurian legends—Tintagel and Merlin's Cave, the Dozmary Pool, Avalon and Glastonbury. We learned about passage tombs and the Book of Kells, how to operate strange showers, accepted that Cornwall's coastal footpath is never level, that Devon's moors are always misty and after a second week there, we realized that there's no place like home.

Most of you know that I had unexpected cancer surgery in November. After coming home from our September Elderhostel, Dann had hernia surgery that we had previously scheduled for October, but in November I went for my annual physical checkup. Dann barely managed time for convalescence before I underwent surgery to remove an abdominal growth. My physicians assured me this might be nothing, but it had to be removed. That was not the case. They removed the remainder of my female organs plus two borderline malignant growths. As they were still self-contained and could be removed I didn't need further treatment. My anesthesiologist commented the next day that my decision to take the time for that annual check-up was a lifesaving decision. My friends all say "but I didn't know you were even sick."

I wasn't and I felt fine (before the surgery at least) so I always responded with "and how long since you've had a check-up?"

When I realized what was up-coming, I looked at my calendar and removed all responsibilities for six weeks. Every time I backed off a responsibility I had to explain to the person who was taking over for me, who then informed the whole organization. As a result, although Dann became kitchen master for a month, food appeared at the door so rapidly that the problem was mostly how much time to give the microwave or where are the proper pans. All that food, plus many flowering plants (people know I have a mini-green house) finally brought home to me how much people were worrying about me. When I complain about lack of energy, my friends hush me firmly. First, they said this would take four weeks of convalescence, and then it changed to six weeks, and then a year. I tell people I can do anything, but I can't do it all. So I'm learning to prioritize.

CHAPTER 35

Seeing Double

March 1, 1998

Dear Cousins,

We now own up to a new (to us) car that we've waited six months to use. Perusing through his catalogs Michael found a '95 Taurus in Montana that had been totaled with extensive rear damage. Next he located a Taurus back clip (this means a car with front damage) here in Wisconsin. He and Dann have been putting the two together since last spring. Dann care-fully moved all the wiring in the damaged rear carefully laying the wires up front to preserve the connections. After welding the two halves together, they reversed the process. We now proudly drive a low mileage, crimson red, '95 Taurus that looks like it just rolled out of the factory. Mike cheerfully allows his Dad to putter in his body shop. Dann does all the elementary work, but when he needs help they work together. They created a beauty and no, I don't worry that the car will come apart when we drive down the road.

We're buried under a three-day snowstorm—too bad, Dorothy, that you're missing it. As I watch the snowflakes lazily drifting down, I picture you on vacation sweltering in the desert.

Last Christmas we gave bread makers to all four sons' families. This year I rated one and have been experimenting frequently. I pour in the proper amount of everything, plug it in and four hours later the smell of fresh homemade bread wafts through the house bringing back memories of many hours mixing and kneading. I used to mix the dough and carry it with me to the office thus giving it time to rise. It sat on the back desk until it traveled home with me at noon for the finishing process in my kitchen

April 6, 1998

Dear Cousins,

I chuckled over Dorothy's description of the big snowstorm and her comment that nobody she knew was in it. Guess who? Dann has cousins in Corning, New York that we've visited often, gone camping, canoeing and skiing with over the years. John Paul and Toby don't have children so they fussed over ours. A year ago John Paul slipped on the ice causing compression of his back vertebrae and she has beginning Alzheimer's so they are staggering under double trouble. We drove out last year to check on them and again this year. He is 88 and she 81. After packing up Monday morning to come home, coming down to breakfast we discovered horror stories on the kitchen TV with pictures of what was occurring right then NW Indiana and Chicago. We know enough about Chicago and snow and what it does to traffic to steer clear, so we promptly unpacked and visited for another 24 hours. Coming home the next day we did okay until we reached the NW corner of Indiana where traffic on Hwy 80 simply stopped. Occasionally we would move a few feet, but snow kept blowing off the lake inhibiting vision. Dann hopped up onto the running board of the semi adjacent to us and the truck driver related the road problems ahead—a whiteout approaching us and a semi that had jack-knifed.

We amused ourselves for three hours listening to our audio book (while worrying about the battery), gnawing on sugared grapefruit strips and Rice Krispie bars, getting frequent reports from the trucker and watching a young couple making out in the car ahead. I desperately wished I hadn't indulged in that half can of Coke when I saw the trucker empty a small can out his window. The radio kept advising that the area around us had been without electricity for three days and Dann pointed out that gas pumps work on electricity. Fortunately our tank was full and we couldn't get to a station anyway. The storm swung right around the southern shore of Lake Michigan.

I agree with Lorraine that grandparenting can get pretty strenuous. Dann and I are struggling to survive spring break. We had two days to rest after Corning before we traveled to Stillwater, Minnesota to stay with Jay's kids, who were on spring break and their Dad was out of town on a business trip. I took the two younger ones to the mall to shop for Elara's birthday present. Trevor and Elara jumped out of the car and raced into the store. I followed at a more sedate pace, locked the car and then stood there wondering about that humming noise. You got it—my keys were still in the ignition and the motor was running. Following the kids into the store I called Grandpa as he carried a second key in his pocket. Of course he had no car and didn't know where I was or how far away. He said he would come, but mentioned gently that I should look for a squad car. As Allison was there with him and as it was she who had given me directions I suggested he ask her how to find us.

When an officer from the sheriff's department happened to walk into the store she gave us a number to call, but when I called to repeat that to Dann, Allison said he had already left riding a less than adult-size bike. I told Elara she had lots of time to decide which two beanie babies she wanted. What I didn't realize was that Allison had directed us to the St. Croix mall, but we had ended up at the Market Place Mall because we reached it sooner. I had told Dann that we were across from the Target store. Dann must have had Divine guidance as although his directions were for the St. Croix, he spotted that Target store and turned into the Market Place Mall. The sheriff arrived right after Dann; we loaded the bike into the car and called it a day. This definitely added to the week's excitement with grandparents. When we told this story to Mike he asked if I had used the electronic code. We have a keyless lock on our new car that can be opened by pushing the five letter code. Unfortunately none of us knew that and it hadn't been set. From now on I only drive cars with keyless locks.

Immediately after we got home from Minnesota we picked up two of Andy's kids, also on spring break. This, too, was a fun time although Dann said in bewilderment "I haven't got anything done all week," and we're exhausted. We had our other half-year birthday party while they were here. I narrow birthday parties to twice a year. Each one covers four months and I get to pick the date. This one covered February, March, April and May, nine of us. Again I made a big 14-inch cake that the kids decorated with names and both Madison families came for supper.

Shortly after we got our two grandchildren tucked in bed, we received a desperate call from Corning from friends of John Paul and Toby. John had been hospitalized with another stroke leaving Toby alone in the house and she refused to move to a residential facility. As long as we had to return our Delavan kids by noon the next day, we decided if we just kept on driving we could reach Corning in a day and a half. Fortunately Dann's brother in Connecticut could get there sooner. Toby keeps saying she doesn't want to be pushed, but I think the decision will be made for her and then the fur will fly. Their house, as big as our old one, is filled with things accumulated for many years and now somebody will have to sort all their belongings. When we moved out of our big house It took us a year to sort and eliminate. I had declared that I would never do that again—but I was wrong.

Yes, Georgiana, I have been working on a story about Grandpa Hibbard and I need you to go with me to the Wisconsin Historical library to check out some dates. Andy has given me Family Tree software as he's eager for me to get my notes organized and entered on the computer.

CHAPTER 36

In Sickness and In Health

June 1, 1998

Dear Cousins,

Most of you know that our Tim underwent brain surgery for the removal of a tumor. This came as a shock to us. He was playing cards at their kitchen island counter with his eight year-old daughter. She tells us that Daddy said "oh" and collapsed. Tim's wife called us from the emergency room and we sat with her through hours of tests. When the MRI showed a tumor they sent him home to wait a week for the surgery. That was a long week. All three of Tim's brothers came 24 hours preceding and stayed for 48 hours afterward. The tumor proved to be benign and it was surgically removed. Tim came out of the recovery room wiggling all his fingers and toes triumphantly. He even worked a couple hours last week. He cannot drive and as this is our busiest season that causes problems. Dann and I have put in extra office time, but it looks as though we scooted through a potential catastrophe and came out okay. Half the city of Madison was praying fervently for us for which we will be forever grateful.

At the time this happened we were scheduled to go back to Corning for another week to help Dann's cousins. We put that on hold momentarily, but eventually we did go and have just now returned back home. John Paul and Toby have been moved to a senior care facility. They leave behind a house filled to capacity. Sad that this came so late that we can no longer ask them how they want to dispose of their things. Toby has apparently been covering up her memory discrepancies for years so now we begin to understand the great accumulation of trash mail. She threw nothing away and we uncovered huge piles of Corning Ware and bedding purchases still sealed. She must have bought presents, but five minutes later couldn't remember what she had purchased. Eight of us worked for 4 ½ days starting with a full attic that we relayed down. I have always claimed to be allergic to dust. Apparently not, as we lived in a virtual dust storm for days and nights and I was fine. Toby may not have remembered what she had, but John's nature was also to collect. When I went through boxes of dusty cancelled checks his mother had written in 1922, I rebelled. However we did save the intriguing 1922 state income taxes. Dann packed every corner of our station wagon and we drove home with an antique bedroom set (the bed strapped on top and the marble top dresser inside), four boxes of uncatalogued genealogy materials (because John Paul was our family historian and now this has all passed to me) and two boxes of sewing equipment destined for clinics in Nicaragua. It was sad to see two people who had been so active, now unable to communicate. We fervently hope we never have to clean out another house.

Attending church while there, I enjoyed the children's sermon about measurements. The pastor showed a yardstick and a scale. He said the scale belonged to a fisherman, but one day a doctor borrowed it to weigh a new baby and it surprised him when the baby weighed 40 lbs. I think the older congregation perhaps enjoyed that story more than the children.

We are preparing for the Wisconsin sesquicentennial. I coordinated a bus tour on the Chief Blackhawk War Trail last month; we visited the Civil War encampment at Camp Randall and we hope to catch the wagon train for their evening camp-fire. They started a week ago in Prairie du Chien with 25 wagons, 100 outriders—all in historic dress, traveling the Old Military Road to Green Bay—234 miles in 16 days at an average of three miles/hour.

August 16, 1998

Dear Cousins,

You all know my brother, Frank, was diagnosed with leukemia. They gave him a time frame of one-three years and encouraged him to take the trip already planned to England and Amsterdam, but he had to be hospitalized while traveling in England. With such a low level of white cells he has no immunity and he picked up an infection. Last week we stayed with Jay's kids in Stillwater, but checked daily on Frank. Coming home Sunday night we unpacked, repacked for Appleton and left again. We returned home that night, but told Lois we could be back in three hours if she needed us. I accompanied them to the doctor's office and he stopped Frank's medication and shifted him to Hospice Home Care. I expect to go back soon.

Although I said in my last letter that Tim was doing okay, his body rejected his meds which sent us often to the emergency room. Now after two months things have improved allowing him to work full time.

October 28, 1998

Dear Cousins,

Lois is doing well. She goes to grief counseling. It helps that she lives in senior housing where friends surround her at all hours. Frank had faced this early and accepted it. For Lois, it was harder. She said that my brother had wanted me to speak at his funeral, payback time because he had sung at our wedding. One can't say no to something like that. All our sons were surprised to hear me speak at the service and surprised also at the stories about my brother. One son said this impressed him so much that he determined to go home and do something to make a difference. Funerals often have this effect on people.

We are still optimistic that Tim will be okay eventually, but apparently recovery from any brain injury takes a long time and the brain reacts to this insult of surgery with seizures. With every additional seizure they change his medication level as trial and error seems to be the only way. Two days before leaving for our Vermont trip, he suffered two bad seizures in one day so we unpacked and stayed home. Tim hurt his shoulder during one seizure and chipped the bone, allowing the ball to slip out of the shoulder joint.

All this made an extremely busy fall, but we needed to get away and relax so drove to Branson, Missouri. This was a first for us as we are apprehensive about crowds and loud music, but we survived. Taking in seven shows in four days all that tremendous talent held us spellbound. We saw the "Shoji Tabuchi" show and the scuttlebutt is right—one mustn't miss strolling through that fabulous bathroom.

As this is teacher's convention, it is Grandparent week again. Today we have Mike's daughter and his dog, tomorrow we get Andy's two kids and later we will add Tim's daughter. Grandpa shakes his head at this, but he enjoys it.

December 29, 1998

Dear Cousins,

I don't know why this robin always lands here right at Christmas. We're in the middle of the holidays as we celebrate four separate Christmases with four sons. The Minnesota one waits until New Year's weekend. Adding three more special Christmas gatherings with two brothers families and another with Lois, makes seven opportunities to rejoice and give thanks for our blessings.

Dear Cousins

We have become involved with Nicaraguan relief. Wisconsin and Nicaragua have been partner states for 30 years so a structure is already in place. Our 400 Dane County Homemakers have been assisting in setting up sewing clinics that teach the women to sew for profit and personal use. We put out a long list of the stuff needed—both material remnants and any supplies or equipment. I had 300 used zippers turn up on my doorstep. I had mistakenly thought only I ripped zippers from worn-out clothes. We sorted everything and packed in half-bushel size boxes, took them to Stevens Point and filled a warehouse. From there National Guard planes, when available, delivered everything to Nicaragua. Hundreds of boxes have been sent. Forty sewing clinics have been established.

As New Year's Eve draws near I can't resist reflecting on this diversified year. We enjoyed constant grandchildren: who played duets with me, climbed our trees, messed up my kitchen with Halloween cookies, meddled with my computer until it only spoke French, beat us frequently at Spite and Malice, one who performed Scottish dances with us and one who achieved the Scout rank of Eagle. We thrilled to dancing with the Scottish demo team whether on the street or on the stage. We suffered through one more house-emptying as we demolished the 40 years of living we found inside our cousin's house. We agonized when we threw away two tons of memories. We realized anew how much we enjoy people as we hosted eight bed and breakfast guests from our senior citizen Evergreen Bed and & Breakfast swap. We studied Wisconsin's sesquicentennial and learned about Victorian dress, the Point of Beginning from whence all Wisconsin land descriptions were surveyed, heard about the problems of early public health when people neither realized nor accepted the importance of quarantine, chatted with travelers on the Wagon Train, and enjoyed musicals portraying life 150 years ago when Wisconsin became the 30th star.

At a state convention this year one speaker raised the question "What one thing do you think people will say about you when you're gone?" We hope it's not "those guys left a lot of junk," but rather "we've done so many inspiring things that provided us with endless memories." So Happy New Year to all of you with wishes for a New Year filled with good health, everlasting peace and warm love. Come see us. We're waiting to make more memories.

February 28, 1999

Dear Cousins,

I constantly play around with my new computer. It has many possibilities and I need the practice. Unfortunately sometimes I try things that I can't stop. With no school yesterday Andy's two kids visited for a couple days. Ten-year-old Aaron always asks to use the computer and when I came in to check he had a crazy overall design on my monitor. He didn't know what he had done and I didn't know how to remove it. When I called his father Andy said, "Oh yeah, he plays around all the time and the last time he crashed my whole system. I couldn't get it running again for two weeks." I am afraid to experiment because I know how easily I get into serious trouble, but these kids try anything.

What a day Sunday has been—so far. We had birthdays approaching for a son and a granddaughter so we offered to take them out to breakfast. Normally we have choir practice at 9:00 a.m. followed by church at 10:00. I called one choir member asking her to tell the choir director that we would be there, but a bit late. We walked in at 9:30 to a reception committee impatiently waiting at the door. The regular organist had the flu and had notified the church at 9:00. Although they knew we were coming they were working into a state of panic. That left me 20 minutes to go over the music the choir was singing, practice twice over the strange African hymn that was on the program and think about what to do for prelude, offertory and postlude. I certainly wished that we hadn't snuck in that special breakfast. I could have used that 30 minutes. Afterwards the treasurer offered me an envelope containing a check. I refused because I hadn't spent any time practicing. He asked, "Are you sure? What about all the stress and strain?"

I told him, "Whatever you've got in that envelope is not enough to cover the stress and strain for this Sunday service."

Dann and I worked at the polls last week. Things proceeded slowly and one teacher thought we needed entertaining so she brought in a sheet entitled "Tips on love from those who should know". All the questions were answered by kids aged five to ten. This relieved our boredom for a long time, but I will repeat only two.

Question: What is the proper age to get married?

(1)"Eighty-four. Because at that age, you don't have to work anymore and you can spend all your time loving each other in your bedroom." Judy, 8 years.

(2)"Once I'm done with kindergarten I'm going to find a wife." Tom aged 5.

CHAPTER 37

Call Home

APRIL 21, 1999

Dear Cousins,

I'm getting this off in record time—less than 24 hours. Necessary as we will shortly be taking off for our second trip with the Friendship Force—this time traveling to Germany. We will be doing home stays—the first week with a family in East Germany (formerly behind the Wall) and the second week in Freiberg near the Black Forest. We are frantically reading German phrase books. I think my capacity may be six words (yes, no, coffee, tea, bathroom and *nein, ich spreche nicht Deutsch*). All with the wrong accent, of course.

Mike and his daughter, Michelle, have just returned from a two week tour in Europe with the Verona High School Music Dept. They performed ten concerts. The logistics of 80 kids traveling accompanied by 30 chaperones floors me. When we saw them off Mike told me he didn't think he was comfortable traveling with 80 teenagers. They did okay except they were close by when trouble broke out in Kosova. They visited the Czech Republic, Vienna, Austria and Germany, where they ran into anti-American riots in Salzburg. They toured a German concentration camp and spent their last days in Paris, running into more anti-American riots. They took off their Verona High School windbreakers at that point because those jackets identified them as Americans. Quite an educational experience for those kids!

On April 10, Tony turned 21. As we have often done with our grandchildren we took him out to eat for his birthday. We were bubbling with enthusiasm for our forthcoming Friendship Force trip to East Germany and between bites as Tony worked his way through an enormous platter of twenty-one golden deep-fried shrimp, he talked about his new welding job. We were delighted that something was working out for him and when we dropped him off at a friend's, we discovered that even at 21, Tony was not too old for hugging. Imprinted on my memory is that thank you and big bear hug that both of us received.

June 20, 1999

Dear Cousins,

And no, you're not going to get a happy tale about our trip to Germany. I think you all know already what happened. We flew non-stop from O'Hare to Frankfurt. Traveling east makes a short night. We lost seven hours between supper and breakfast, making me wonder when that plane goes to bed. I thought this beats the way our grandparents crossed the ocean. The journey had many legs all of which got longer and longer—a delayed takeoff at O'Hare, a three-hour wait in the Frankfurt terminal going through Passport Control, delayed baggage claim in Leipzig because one bag went astray and transportation in three rented vans via the Autobahn to Jena. Gradually hosts appeared in the parking lot and one by one they picked us up. We were housed with a delightful young family complete with *OOma* (grandma) and ten year-old Sebastian. Our German was passable only if we worked at it. Petra and Gunther had an electronic translator which helped. *OOma* has a separate apartment where we slept. She has Alzheimer's, which made for exciting living as without notice she would wander in and out of our bedroom and bath. She spoke in complete sentences rapidly that defeated us. The most crucial word that afternoon was Dann's *"schlafen mit Frau"* as he indicated that we needed a nap.

Our hosts adapted their working hours to make themselves available and drove us throughout the countryside. Castles perch on every ridge and we climbed endlessly. We spent five exciting days sightseeing, but especially looked forward to Mother's Day, also observed in Germany. Caravaning with three cars we set off for Dresden to view the palace grounds, the ancient residence of the king and to tour the Zwinger. After a long day of wonderful sightseeing, we piled back into the car, but as we were driving down the Autobahn the car phone rang and the voice of our trip leader echoed throughout the car, "Someone is trying to reach the Willett's. Please call home immediately." By the time we had driven back to our apartment E-mail messages were coming through, "Call home." We knew of only one reason why our family would try to reach us and both of us silently considered each family member as we waited and waited for that return call to go through. Was it an older brother who had been having dizzy spells? Or our son who had been struggling since his brain surgery? Or perhaps one of the family in the Twin Cities because it was that son who was trying to reach us? When the call finally came through, Jason told us that Tony had been out with friends the night before celebrating his 21st birthday. Because those friends had been drinking he had said that he could not ride with them and would jog home. Tony had done cross-country running in high school so jogging five miles down a country road would not be difficult. It was 2:00 a.m. and he was almost home. A car going in the same direction as Tony flashed its lights at oncoming cars to alert them to possible danger on the road. As three cars approached, the first slowed in response to the warning. A pickup truck, second in line, impatiently sped up passed the first car and swerved killing Tony instantly. The woman driver panicked and left. When the police picked her up three hours later her blood alcohol level still tested at 1.34. Tony did the right thing, but it put him in the wrong place at the wrong time. He did jog home that night, but not to the home he knew.

Petra immediately asked for our tickets and faxed a copy to the travel agent in Leipzig. In rapid German Petra and Gunther explored our options deciding that we couldn't get out that night. We held group tickets. We could no longer go forward with the group, but had to retrace our steps to Leipzig to return to Frankfurt for the international lap. Reservations were changed, discounted tickets were undiscounted. We made another call to Tony's home in Delavan where we learned that Tony's father had been awakened at 6:30 a.m. that morning by the police. Andy had made one call to his brother in Madison asking if he could locate Mom and Dad. Both Madison brothers with their wives then left immediately for Delavan after asking their out-of-state brother to wait by his phone for us to "call home". On our way to bed that night, I picked up the nine postcards that Dann had written to our grandchildren. Tony's, ready for mailing, rested on top.

After a night of tossing and turning, 6:00 a.m. finally arrived. Gunther took off from work to drive us to the Leipzig airport. Petra's contact person of the night before was working on our problems. She walked us to the Money Express where we dumped our pockets—using first our Deutsche traveler's checks and Deutschmarks, then our American traveler's checks and then cash as we bought a ticket for the Leipzig to Frankfurt segment and paid the penalty for changing from the group discounted tickets. Gunther stayed with us until our luggage was checked through and we held boarding passes. Because Leipzig could not give us seats together, they had told us to explain at the boarding gate in Frankfurt and request a change. We did this and after much chattering in German, we boarded and found ourselves together in the business section complete with back massages and hot towels.

Everything happened so rapidly I think we did not realize the extent of our loss until we breezed through customs in Chicago and in the midst of that solid mass of people waiting for people; we spotted two familiar ones with tears streaming down their faces.

We felt heavily indebted to Petra and Gunther for enabling us to return home so rapidly. When I had tried to thank her, she paged through the phrase book until she came to "naturally". I think she meant that naturally a Friendship Force friend helps another in time of need.

We learned much from Tony as we had attempted to fill his life with love and learning experiences. Tony had faced many problems in his life and had received a huge amount of grandparent exposure. Perhaps it was ordained that we had needed to cram a lifetime into 21 years. I think we made a difference in his life and he in ours. His father asked me to say something at the funeral. As I faced the congregation that day I saw tears streaming down the faces of Tony's friends, the ones who had been drinking that night and thus had been unable to give him a ride home. I fervently hoped this might influence their future decisions. At home that night I stared at the half-dozen bottles of wine on our pantry shelf. It seemed so fruitless—one person's night out having a good time in exchange for the life of another. I carried the bottles to the kitchen sink and amidst a deluge of tears streaming down my face; I opened and poured it all down the drain. Never again will we either partake of or serve any alcoholic beverage in our home.

I like to think that perhaps Tony's legacy might save someone else's life. I am humbly grateful for the many prayers all of you dear cousins fielded in our direction. If you see a twinkling star in the heavens you may be looking at a star with a new name (Anthony Dann Willett) located at Hydra 14th-25.8 degrees.

I had thought grandparenting would be easy. Not so. Grandparents have to laugh when things may not be funny and cry when they are tragic, have to be mean and make rules and stick to them, have to find time to do things that may seem irrelevant, have to be patient and understanding and give advice that probably isn't going to be taken, and have to be repetitive because none of them listen the first few times or understand that they will make bad judgments. They need to know that they learn by those mistakes and we love them anyway. We've been in training for many years and will continue learning how to be caring, supportive grandparents as we search out the joys of retirement, but our lives will always continue to be a series of hills and valleys.

EPILOGUE

Retirement is best described as continuing to do what you have always done, but only when you feel like doing it. Our retirement created a challenge as we continued to work off and on, interspersed with the presence of frequent grandchildren and far flung trips, which fulfilled our dreams of exploring the world and allowed us to develop a love for all people and a better understanding of diverse cultures. What started out as a story on grandchildren soon became a story of how to fill one's retirement years with much more. Even in retirement we couldn't find enough time to fulfill all our dreams.

Although the grandchildren still play an important part of our lives, we see less of them as they followed our example of searching out learning experiences and are busy pursuing careers in Business Administration, Environmental Science, Evolution and Ecology, Politics, Photography, International language, Computers, Physics and Math. Several widened their horizons by doing semesters abroad in Scotland, Ireland and Hungary. Tony remains forever in our memories as the happy-go-lucky kid, who had to learn everything the hard way, who never outgrew our hugs and who, like his grandfather, charmed everyone with his smile as he willingly tried anything.

Living alongside grandchildren was never boring nor monotonous, just as raising their fathers was never boring nor monotonous. And the combination of filling those retirement years with both grandchildren and travel abroad provided constant continuing education for us and a life that also never became boring nor monotonous.

After close to 60 years the cousin round robin still flies bonding us together as we tell and retell family stories—both exciting new experiences and reminiscing over the stories of yore. It still makes seven stops on each swing because, although two of the original robins are no longer with us, their presence remains as their daughters have stepped into their Moms' footsteps.

Jean Willett's love of children was matched by a love for writing leading into a position as columnist for five years for the Dane County Kids publication. Sending submissions to the Extension Homemakers (now known as Wisconsin Association for Home & Community Education) her short stories won first place at county level and went on to state level earning the Cultural Arts State Medallion for best in show for two consecutive years. She has published in the Wisconsin Academy Review.

In 2005 she published her first book entitled *Dear Mom – Why Raising Four Boys Was Neither Boring nor Monotonous*. *Dear Cousins – Staying Connected the Old Fashioned Way* is the sequel.

Jean Willett, local author born in Delavan, Wisconsin, received a degree in Occupational Therapy from the University of Wisconsin-Madison. She met her husband Dann while on campus and located permanently in Madison. She chose careers that involved children working first in Pediatrics with Rheumatic Fever children facing long term hospitalization. Stopping briefly to have four sons, when the boys reached school age, she trained and worked for the Madison Board of Education as naturalist consultant in the Madison School Forest.

If you have enjoyed this book, feel free to send comments to Jean Willett directly at dannjean@sbcglobal.net

A portion of the proceeds of this book will be donated to M.A.D.D. (MOTHERS AGAINST DRUNK DRIVING)

DIRECTIONS FOR SPITE AND MALICE

Any number of participants is acceptable

It requires two to four decks of cards depending on number of players

Each player receives a STACK—anywhere from 10-15 cards but the same number for each player!) These are placed face down in front of each player with top card face up.

The OBJECT OF THE GAME is to be first using up your entire stack.

Each player is also dealt a hand of five cards.

Piles are built upon in the center -ace low, queen finishes the pile as kings are wild and can be used for anything except aces or queens. Suits do not matter. No more than four piles can be active at the same time.

ON THE FIRST ROUND

Player with the highest face card on his or her stack (kings do not count) plays first and play continues clockwise.

Do not DRAW on this first round.

If you are holding or draw aces it is obligatory to play them UNLESS there are already four on the table. Play whatever you can and end your turn by discarding. You are allowed to build up 4 discard piles next to your stack. These are like money in the bank and can always be used to play on the center piles. If these discards are made in numerical order from high to low, then it is often possible to use a bunch of them at one turn starting with the top card, of course.

It is fun, and helpful to play from the discard piles but remember the object of the game is to use up your stack so always play from there FIRST.

SUBSEQUENT ROUNDS

Always draw first taking your hand up to 5.

If you play your entire hand, without discarding, you may draw an entire new hand immediately. You always end your turn by discarding.

Although playing aces is a requirement, other cards may be held back if one cannot resist being spiteful or full of malice. Therefore, always keep an eye on the top of your opponent's stack and try not to set the center piles up for his play.

Have fun and be nasty.

Printed in the United States
221327BV00001B/6/P